Y0-EGD-793

An Illustrated
Guide to Making
Oriental Rugs

An Illustrated
Guide to Making
Oriental Rugs

by Gordon W. Scott

Pacific Search Press

Pacific Search Press, 222 Dexter Avenue North
        Seattle, Washington 98109
© 1984 by Gordon W. Scott. All rights reserved
Printed in the United States of America

Edited by Leila Charbonneau
Designed by Judy Petry
Illustrations by John Berry
Cover: Gendje mat

Library of Congress Cataloging in Publication Data

Scott, Gordon W.
        An illustrated guide to making oriental rugs.

        Bibliography: p.
        Includes index.
        1. Rugs, Oriental.   2. Hand weaving.   I. Title.
TT850.S38   1984   746.7′5   84-14734
ISBN 0-914718-94-0

Contents

Acknowledgments

I am deeply grateful to the following people who are largely responsible for any success I have had with the process of making Oriental rugs. Harry Jamharian first introduced me to the Tabriz loom and Persian weaving techniques. Bill Knadjian of Albuquerque, New Mexico, and Art Khoury of Amarillo, Texas, are rug dealers of the highest caliber who not only encouraged me in my pursuit, but supplied me with tools and rug designs. Mrs. Karim Pahlevan and her son Asghar have been immensely helpful in providing me with advice, tools, and designs. Dick Ruddy did a fine job on the color plates of the rugs. Kathleen Summers is to be commended for her patience and diligence in transferring rug designs to graph paper for the text. Melissa Howard has been a great help in editing the book and getting it in proper form for publication. I owe her a special thanks. John Berry's dual training in engineering and art made him well suited to illustrate the technical chapters. Finally, I thank my wife Madeline for tolerating my obsession with rugs over the years and for giving advice along the way. Without the help of all these friends, this book would not have been possible.

Glossary

Bubbles: Half-circular segments of weft placed loosely between the warps.

Daftoon: A metal rug beater weighing three to four pounds, used on finer rugs.

Dowels: Wooden poles over which warp is wound.

Gul: A stylized motif in Oriental rugs, often octagonal and repeated at regular intervals in the central part of the rug.

Heading: A flat woven band at the beginning and end of the rug, made of the weft material.

Heddles: Harnesslike devices to pull the back warps forward to create a shed.

Leash sticks: Wide, thin strips of wood the width of the loom inserted between the front and back warps to preserve enough warp to tie later as fringe.

Pile: The upright woolen fibers on the surface of knotted pile rugs.

Rug comb or beater: A wooden or metal implement for compacting the rows of knots.

Selvage: The binding for the sides of the rug.

Shed: A space created between the front and back warps for the passage of weft.

Shed #1: A shed created when the front warps are in front and the back warps are in back.

Shed #2: A shed created when the front warps are in back and the back warps are in front.

Skein: A hank of yarn wound in an orderly fashion.

Umbrella swift: An umbrella-shaped rotary device used to unwind skeins of yarn.

Warp: Longitudinal strings that are wound around the loom, placed under tension, and around which knots are tied.

Weft: The transverse strings that are placed between each row of knots and are insinuated between warp strings.

Introduction

Admired and treasured throughout the world, Oriental rugs have long been an object of fascination for rug importers, antique dealers and collectors, artists, and those of us who appreciate and love fine art or attempt to make it ourselves. To many of us, the actual techniques used to produce a fine Oriental knotted pile rug may be as much of a mystery as the meanings behind the remarkable designs and symbols woven into them.

My aim in this guide is to take the mystery out of making Oriental rugs by illustrating, in detailed steps, how to build a loom and hand-knot an Oriental rug. By using the same methods and materials that have produced such beautiful works of art over the centuries, you can make a rug as fine and intricate as those originating in the Middle East and the Orient.

Knotted pile weaving is different from the well-known tapestry or flat weaving in that knots are tied around pairs of vertical threads, called the warp, leaving a long pile, which must be trimmed even. The fabric is held together by two rows of horizontal threads, called the weft, woven between each row of knots. In flat weaving, the horizontal weft is woven over and under the vertical warp to form a mesh. The weft completely covers the warp.

This technique of knotted pile weaving is believed to have originated among the Mongolian peoples in the East. The earliest fragment of a knotted pile rug, the Pazyryk rug, was discovered in 1947 by a Russian archeologist in a Scythian burial mound near the Russian border of outer Mongolia. Radioactive carbon analysis dates the rug to the fifth century B.C. From Mongolia, knotted pile weaving spread to China, Iran, India, Turkey, and Pakistan. Less well known is the fact that knotted pile weaving also was common in France and England in the sixteenth through the eighteenth centuries. Seventeenth century French Savonnerie and Abusson rugs and eighteenth century English Axminister rugs, found in museums, bear witness to the popularity of this craft in Europe.

Scholars of Oriental rugs speculate that the first knotted pile rugs were woven by nomadic shepherds as utilitarian substitutes for animal skins, which were scarce. These early rugs probably had long pile and were used for warming floors of homes, for saddle and storage bags, and for tent closures.

As tribes began to grow crops and to settle in villages, they learned to dye the wools with substances found in indigenous plants and even insects. Dyed wools allowed them to make colorful designs. The earliest were crude geometric designs that often included replicas of the animals and insects encountered in their daily lives. As larger cities developed, individuals no longer pursued weaving as an after-hours cottage industry, but could be full-time artisans. They enlisted the help of artists and produced designs that represented the lovely flowers so cherished by people of the arid Middle East to this day. These works of art tended to be muted and subtle in color and composition and expressed the city dwellers' love of art. The villager, by contrast, in his harsh, unbelievably drab surroundings, still preferred the garish colors that brightened his gray existence.

The designs and colors used in Oriental knotted pile weaving throughout the Middle East and the Orient are rich and varied. The geometric tribal rugs of the Turkoman and Beluchistan tribes can be recognized by their stylized designs representing crabs, flowers, spiders, and dogs. Rugs from the Caucasus, Turkey, and southern Iran are similar in their use of rams' horns, goats, and sheep, and stylized trees, flowers, and snowflakes. From Iran, there are the garden carpets of Qum, the delicate floral rugs of Kerman and Kashan, and the harsher, more angular floral carpets of Tabriz.

In Iran today, rug making is still a vital part of the culture. One of my colleagues, Dr. Rajaee, a native of Tehran, points out that whatever one says about Persian rug production in one area of Iran is only true for that particular area, for there is great variety and complexity in rug use and production. In Iran, virtually everyone has knotted pile rugs. The poor may have the cheaper, loosely woven woolen rugs, while the well-to-do have the finely knotted ones outlined in silk, such as are made in Isfahan, Tabriz, or Nain.

Thinking back to his childhood in the early 1940s, Dr. Rajaee recalls that rugs were often made at home. The best ones were made by young girls and became part of their dowry. Often rugs were made by the "dokhtere Khane," older girls who had never married—ladies-in-waiting. He recalls that his father said that Reza Shah, father of the Shah who was ousted in 1979, outlawed children working on rugs during school hours and required compulsory education. By the 1940s, few children worked on rugs in the cities. Compulsory education, however, was not well enforced in the villages and a large percentage of the weaving work force still consisted of children.

Dr. Rajaee's chief exposure to village weaving came when, as a boy, he visited with his family in Gonbadeghaboos, a village near Gorgan in northern Iran, just east of the Caspian Sea and near the Russian border. There the Turkoman tribe wove soft, finely knotted geometric rugs, which Americans called Bokharas. Curiously, the men did most of the weaving and the women tended to the sheep and raised the crops. The rugs were made on upright looms in the home. For larger rugs, several families collaborated on a large loom. At one time, the people used their own wool, which they processed and dyed. Gradually, rug dealers supplied wool and materials to the villagers in return for money or a portion of the rugs produced.

Dr. Rajaee's wife, Parvin, recalls an interesting example of rug making in the late 1940s. Her step-grandmother, wife of an army general under Reza Shah and originally of the Luri tribe, lived in the village of Chadegan, near Isfahan. She had looms built for a large room in her house and bought wool and supplies. Village girls would come to her house and work for a few rials (pennies) a day and make large- and medium-size rugs. Most of the rugs were given to family members, but some of the larger ones were sold.

Asghar Pahlevan, whose father was my patient in Albuquerque and whose mother was my weaving mentor, also is from Isfahan. His uncle is a rug designer and has been in the rug business most of his life. When Asghar was in his mid-twenties in 1972, he was involved in rug production in the village of Dasgerd, near Isfahan. Asghar supplied about eighty village homes with needed supplies and designs for pictorial rugs measuring two and a half by four feet. These rugs had approximately 500 knots per square inch. There were two looms in each village home. Asghar paid the labor costs of 600 tomans (about seventy-five dollars) per rug. The materials cost him about thirty-five dollars per rug. Two weavers completed the two carpets in six months. At the end of that time, the family had the choice of keeping one of the two rugs and getting no cash for labor or getting $150 for the six months of work. Most of the weavers took the money. In that area, most villagers could not afford to own knotted pile rugs but instead owned kelims, flat weavings without the pile.

In figures 1 through 5, Asghar Pahlevan's cousin, Esmat Karbassian, is shown working at a traditional village loom.

My entire family learned to love Oriental rugs when we lived in Iran from 1959 to 1964. My job as a surgeon in a mission hospital prevented me from learning about rug production then, but we did collect a number of lovely rugs and brought them back to the United States with us.

In 1974 I had an opportunity to learn how to make Oriental rugs. Harry Jamharian, an Iranian-Armenian patient of mine, was a rug dealer in Albuquerque, New Mexico, and repaired Oriental rugs. He knew how to make an upright loom and was teaching a few students to make knotted pile rugs. Unfortunately, the students were left to create their own designs and were using American rug yarn and rug ends, so the end products bore little resemblance to Oriental rugs. He offered to make a loom for me, to string it, and to show me the basics of tying knots and making a knotted pile rug.

I started a small mat, but was disappointed with the result and put it aside before it was finished. One year later, while I was recovering from an illness, I finished the mat and in the process learned how to string the loom. I then built a larger loom and over the next year made a three-by-five-foot Caucasian rug with a Talish design. I had copied this design by trial and error from pictures in several of my rug books. This particular rug appealed to me because I had had several patients from the Talish district of Iran just south of the Talish district of Caucasian Russia.

The next rug I made was a Turkoman and took a year to complete. It was a great improvement over the first Talish, but there were still many problems with keeping the sides even. It was single wefted, which gave it a limp feeling and a lack of authenticity.

It was at this time that I met Asghar Pahlevan and through him, his mother, Mrs. Pahlevan. Mrs. Pahlevan had made fine rugs in Isfahan from the age of seven until she married at age thirteen. She spent many hours in our home and examined the sample I had on the loom. She was quick to diagnose the principal problems. First, she claimed that my daftoon (an instrument for beating down the rows of knots and wefts) was too small. She promised that when back in Iran she would send me a proper daftoon, some better rug scissors, and some designs for floral rugs. She also showed me how to keep the sides of the rug from pulling in and told me that in Iran they use a thick weft under tension and, with the shed reversed, they use a loosely inserted, soft, thin weft. In about fifteen hours of questioning, I learned more than I had learned in the previous fifteen hundred hours of trial and error weaving. When the Pahlevans returned to Iran, they sent me the promised supplies. This was particularly commendable and amazing, because at the time they mailed the supplies, the revolution was starting and the Shah, an American ally, was being threatened with expulsion. Thanks to their generosity and kindness, I had the tools necessary to make very finely textured rugs in addition to the coarser rugs I made with locally available tools. I still hear from the Pahlevans. They say they pray for me every day (in proper Moslem fashion on a Persian rug).

All that remained for me to do was to locate wool comparable to Persian wool and to make rugs demonstrating the variations on the themes that Mrs. Pahlevan had so compe-

1.

2.

3.

4.

5.

1. *This traditional upright village loom was photographed in a home near Isfahan, Iran, in 1982. It is somewhat crudely constructed, but a master weaver can overcome its shortcomings. Displayed on the box where the weaver will sit while at work are scissors, knives, and a daftoon (beater).*

2. *The weaver, Esmat Karbassian, a cousin of my friend Asghar Pahlevan, examines the pattern for her rug before tying a row of knots. The rug has 500 knots per square inch.*

3. *She holds the knife in the palm of her right hand as she ties the knots. The hook on the end of the knife brings one pair of warp threads to the front so that the pile material can be knotted around them.*

4. *After tying a row of knots and beating it down with a daftoon, the weaver pulls the thick weft in front and beats it in place.*

5. *Next, the thin blue weft comes to the front, where it will be beaten in loosely. All that remains is to cut a row of knots and trim the excess pile with her scissors. Iranians cut the way they write—from right to left—and think the rest of us do it backward.*

tently provided me. This process culminated in the floral Kashan rug (plate I), followed by the Talish (plate H). The Kashan rug has 180 knots per square inch. Three small rugs with woolen warp and weft followed.

As I made these rugs and showed them to friends and co-workers, I was overwhelmed by their response. Dozens of people showed great interest in my hobby and asked me to teach classes. This response convinced me that my hobby does have a general appeal.

The simplicity of the techniques and tools used in knotted pile weaving also convinced me that this hobby is suitable for just about anyone. All the weaver needs is a frame around which he can wind the warp threads, a system for making sheds for passage of the weft, pile yarn for tying knots, some scissors, and a knife. I have located sources for all of the tools and materials needed. With the help of artists and Iranians experienced in weaving, I have put together illustrations and instructions that will enable diligent and persistent readers, with no weaving experience at all, to begin making Oriental knotted pile rugs. For example, Oriental knotted pile weaving is especially well suited for the retired person who has free time and patience, and who is interested in a challenging activity that will result in a rug of beauty and value. The techniques and designs described in this book also will appeal to experienced weavers who admire Oriental rugs and want to broaden their craft, and who have not been able to find specific or sufficient information on this art form.

To my knowledge, there is no book in English that adequately covers all the steps involved in making an Oriental rug. There is little or no information on building and warping a loom, obtaining materials, or actually hand-knotting a rug. My research on this subject in the Museum of Textile Arts in Washington, D.C., led me to uncover only one piece of literature on the subject, a monograph entitled, "Notes on Proper Knotting and Weaving," by C. E. C. Tattersall from the Victoria and Albert Museum. I recommend this monograph as a general reference, but warn that it lacks specific detail and does not provide source information on weaving materials and tools. This monograph can be obtained for approximately two dollars by writing:

Textile Museum
2320 S. Street N.W.
Washington, D.C. 20008

or

Pendragon House, Inc.
220 University Avenue
Palo Alto, California 94301

In the rest of this book you will find:

Instructions for building a loom and tips on buying wool, tools, and supplies.
A chapter on the principles of knotted pile weaving, and the factors that influence a rug's shape, texture, design, and consistency.
Tips for preventing and correcting mistakes.
Instructions for rug construction, including warping the loom, tying the knots, inserting the various types of weft, weaving the selvage and the headings, and making the fringe.
Detailed instructions for a sample rug.
Nine designs and photographs for making your own rug, as well as instructions on materials and techniques, and comments on colors and designs.
A source list for scissors, beaters, and materials for warp, weft, and pile.*
A list of recommended books on Oriental rugs.

If you use all the designs, which are provided in this book, you will be kept busy and most likely enthralled for many years to come. But it all begins with a single, simple step. So enjoy!

---

* The texture of the rugs made with the wool recommended here is superior to that of the average Iranian, Indian, or Turkish rug. After you learn how to make rugs with about eighty knots per square inch you will need authentic Middle Eastern tools to progress to rugs of finer quality up to two hundred knots per square inch.

CHAPTER 1

Looms, Tools, and Materials

Weaving in the United States is usually done on sophisticated and often expensive looms. It surprises most American weavers to learn that the lovely and complicated rugs of the Middle East and Orient are woven on very simple looms. (See figs. 1 through 5.)

Types of looms

In the Orient there are four types of looms generally used for constructing knotted pile rugs.

Horizontal loom. The simplest loom is the lightweight horizontal one used by nomadic tribal groups. Although the design of the loom requires that the weaver work in what looks like an uncomfortable squatting position, the loom suits the nomadic existence of its users. It consists of two horizontal beams around which the warp is wound, creating two sheds. The wound loom is placed on the ground and tension is established and maintained by driving stakes into the ground. The stakes force the upper and lower beams farther apart and maintain tension on the warps. Because the loom must be used in the weaver's small tent dwelling, the size of rugs is limited. Each time the family moves to better grazing areas, the loom, with the partly completed rug still on it, must be taken up. If you examine rugs made by nomadic groups, you will often see variation in the height of the repetitive designs. Longitudinal undulations are not uncommon on the surface of the carpet because of the difficulty in reestablishing the same tension on the warps when the loom is set up in a new location. (Looser tension results in fewer vertical rows of knots per inch and a taller design. Areas of the rug woven with less tension on the warps have longitudinal ripples.)

Vertical loom. The village vertical loom is an upright variation of the horizontal loom. The two horizontal beams, instead of being on the ground and thrust apart by stakes, are attached to two vertical beams. The upper horizontal beam is stationary and the lower one is movable in a slot.

Tension is adjusted by driving wedges between the top of the movable beam and the top of the slot in which it rests.

An Iranian friend of mine described the winding of such a loom from firsthand experience. Two strong, straight poles are driven into level ground. The distance between the poles determines the length of the rug to be made on the loom. A third pole is driven into the ground midway between the two end poles. All of these poles are perpendicular to the ground, in a straight line, and of equal height above the ground.

The weaver ties the warp thread to an end pole close to the ground. The warp is then wound on one side of the center pole, around the other end pole, on the opposite side of the center pole and back to the point of origin. The winding continues in a circular fashion around the poles so that at completion the end poles are covered with concentric turns of warp one layer thick. The center pole keeps the front and back warps separated for later shed formation.

When the poles are wound with the desired number of warps, they are removed from the ground. One of the end poles is tied with strong wires to the movable lower horizontal beam of a vertical loom. The space between the warps is maintained with the center pole. The warp loops are taken off the second end pole two pairs at a time and are tied under uniform tension like shoestrings over the fixed horizontal beam. Because the end poles were much farther apart than the height of the vertical loom, a long length of warps hangs down from the upper horizontal beam where the warps are tied. The heddles are tied and then the warp pairs are carefully spaced to give the desired number per inch. Tension is increased by driving the wedges in above the movable lower beam. When the weaving has progressed close to the heddles, all the warps have to be untied from the upper beam and the rug pulled down and nailed to the front surface of the lower beam. A leather strap is used to nail the rug to the lower beam. The warps are retied to the upper beam and tension is reestablished.

The weaving continues until the space below the heddles is used up. Then the nails are removed from the leather strap and the warps are untied from the upper beam. The rug is moved down and renailed to the lower beam. This tedious tying and untying of the warps is a great disadvantage of this loom. Another drawback is that as the weaving progresses the weaver must sit on a progressively higher seat until the rug is moved down, and then the seat must be lowered. .

Tabriz loom. The Tabriz loom is a great improvement over the horizontal loom or the upright village loom. This is the one I have elected to use and it is described in detail in this chapter.

Roller loom. The roller loom is used in the cities of Kerman, Kashan, and Isfahan and in other cities where large rugs are made. Essentially the warps are wound around a roller beam at the top of the loom and stretched to the lower beam. As the rug is completed, it is wound around the lower beam. The weaver can sit at one level and move the rug down as the weaving progresses.

The Tabriz loom

The Tabriz loom is ideally suited for the home weaver. It is constructed and wound so that as the rug is woven it can be progressively moved to the back side of the loom. A rug can be made that is slightly smaller than two times the distance between the upper and lower horizontal beams.

The basic form of the Tabriz loom is simple. Two vertical beams are constructed so that they have slots cut to insert upper, middle, and lower horizontal beams. Either the top or the bottom horizontal beam is movable in the slot, which is longer than the height of the movable beam. This mobility in the slot allows for the tension on the warps to be relaxed during movement of the rug to the back of the loom. Dowels placed on the front of the vertical beams allow the formation of sheds. When the weaving approaches the heddles, tension can be relaxed and the rug slid to the back of the loom so that the leading edge of the rug (the edge being woven) is just above the lower horizontal beam. Then the tension is reestablished and the rug nailed to the lower beam under a leather strap.

There are two basic kinds of Tabriz looms. Choice depends on concern for expense, availability of power tools, and aesthetic considerations.

The loom with the movable lower horizontal beam (loom 1) can be built with hand tools (although an inexpensive saber saw facilitates cutting the slots). The cost in materials is less than $20. It will look like rough carpentry, much like the village Tabriz looms in Iran or Turkey.

The loom with the movable upper beam (loom 2) requires power tools such as a router, power saw, and drill press. If you have to hire the work done, it will cost between $75 and $100, including materials. But power tools will ensure that the joints are perfect and the surfaces smooth. More important, the mechanical device for increasing the tension on the warps will be more efficient.

Medium-grade white pine is satisfactory construction material for both looms. There is no need for hardwood for the loom, but hardwood (oak or walnut) is generally more satisfactory for the wedges used with loom 1.

Tabriz loom with movable lower beam (Loom 1)

The first type of Tabriz loom, with the movable lower beam, is the one I am most experienced with. Tension is established by driving wedges in above the lower horizontal beam. The advantage of this loom is that it can be built with hand tools even if you have little experience in carpentry. The disadvantage is that reestablishing tension on the warps requires a hydraulic jack (one can be purchased for about $15). Because a jack 4 inches wide is needed to thrust the lower beam downward, there must be a 4-inch clearance on either side for the jack and for manipulation of the wedges. Thus the maximum width of a rug made on this loom is about 4 inches narrower than a rug made on the loom with a movable upper beam (loom 2), even though both looms are the same width. I have made several good looms with hand tools and can testify to their efficiency.

6. *Tabriz loom 1 with movable lower beam, side view (See fig. 24 on p. 23 for a two-dimensional view of finished loom.)*

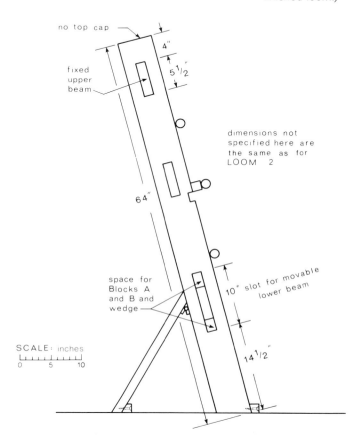

no top cap

fixed upper beam

4"

5 1/2"

dimensions not specified here are the same as for LOOM 2

64"

space for Blocks A and B and wedge

10" slot for movable lower beam

14 1/2"

SCALE: inches
0   5   10

Loom parts. The dimensions of the loom are shown in figures 6 and 7. As you look at the front and side views you will see that the loom consists of the following features:

1. Two vertical beams (2 x 6s) with slots for the upper and middle fixed beams and a slot for the movable lower beam
2. Three horizontal beams (2 x 6s)—upper, middle, and lower
3. One brace across the lower front portion of the vertical beams and a second brace across the back legs
4. Legs and braces to support the loom (an angled hinged brace or chains can be used to prevent overextension of the legs)
5. Two blocks in position C
6. Blocks A and B for both sides of the lower beam (fig. 8)
7. Wedges for both sides of the lower beam (fig. 8)
8. Dowel 1 to be nailed in position A
9. Dowel 2 to be nailed in position B
10. Dowel 3 rounded on the end for insertion into the shed
11. Spacer S to go in between dowel 1 and the middle beam (fig. 8)

Figure 8 shows the dimensions and configurations of spacer S. The construction of this spacer may be difficult for you. An alternative method to prevent upward bending of dowel 1 during warping is to place a pliable heavy twine around dowel 1, under the lower horizontal beam, and tighten it snugly. Slide this along as you warp the loom and this will prevent bowing of dowel 1.

Materials for loom 1 (figs. 6 and 7). (2 x 6s available in 6-, 8-, 10-, 12-, and 14-foot lengths)

Two 6-foot pine 2 x 6s
Three 4-foot pine 2 x 6s
Three 4-foot pine 2 x 2s (make blocks for position C from scrap 2 x 2s)
Three 4-foot dowels, 1¼ inches in diameter (very straight)
One 12-inch pine lathe, ½ x ½ inch
Two card table hinges
Fifteen 4-inch #12 screws
Fifteen 2-inch #10 screws
Ten #8 box nails
Ten #10 box nails

Materials for spacer S, blocks A and B, and wedges (fig. 8).

One 4-foot oak 3 x 1¼
One 3-foot piece of heavy twine if not using spacer S
Power saw

7. Tabriz loom 1 with movable lower beam, front view

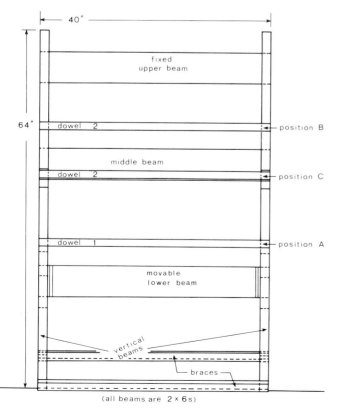

(all beams are 2 x 6s)

SCALE: inches
0   5   10

8. Scale drawing of wedge, blocks A and B, and spacer S (See fig. 25 on p. 24 for a two-dimensional view of wedge, blocks, and Spacer S.)

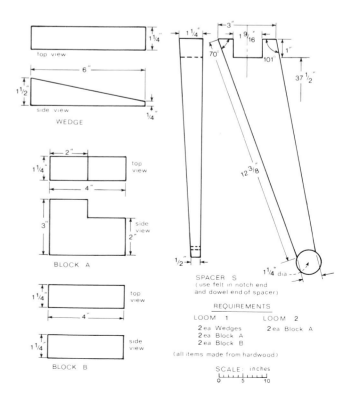

Assembly instructions. Tabriz loom 1 is constructed in the following way:

Step 1: Cut the 2 x 6s in the indicated length and shape for the two vertical beams.

Step 2: In the vertical beams cut slots as indicated for the upper, middle, and lower horizontal beams. Slots can be cut with hand tools. First drill half-inch holes with a brace and bit at the top, bottom, and center of the slot. Use either a saber saw or a keyhole saw to saw out the slots the same size as the 2 x 6 that will be inserted into the slot. Finish off the slots with a file so that the 2 x 6 fits snugly into the slot. Make sure that the slots for the lower horizontal beam are large enough for free movement of the lower horizontal beam upward and downward. Cut notches just below position C in front of vertical beams. This is to facilitate passage of a shuttle through the shed.

Step 3: Cut the three horizontal beams the length indicated in the plans. Cut the lower brace for the bottom of the front of the vertical beams, and cut the back legs and the brace to go across the bottom of the back legs. Use a plane and then sandpaper to round off the sharp edges at the top of the upper beam and at the bottom of the lower beam, front and back. This will prevent fraying and breaking of warp thread later on.

Step 4: Drill two holes through the back of each vertical beam at the midpoint of the slots for the upper and middle horizontal beams. Of course, all holes should be slightly smaller than the screw or nail used. The hole goes through the back of the vertical beam into the slot. Also drill the holes that will hold the braces on the front of the bottom of the vertical beams and back legs as shown.

Step 5: Insert the upper, middle, and lower horizontal beams into the slots so that the ends are flush with the outside of the vertical beams on each side. While the beams are held in this position, deepen the screw holes made in the back of the vertical beams so that they go into the middle and upper horizontal beams. Now insert 4-inch No. 12 screws to fix the upper and middle horizontal beams securely. Use 2-inch No. 10 screws to fasten the braces across the bottom of the front of the vertical beams and across the bottom of the back legs.

Step 6: Nail two 6-inch-long ½ x ½-inch pieces of lathe to the front sides of the movable lower beam ¼ inch inside the vertical beams to prevent lateral movement of this beam in the slot.

Step 7: Attach legs with 2-inch No. 10 screws to the position shown in the plans.

Step 8: Drill holes for nailing dowel 1 to position A (to be nailed in place later). This position should allow spacer S (if it is used) to fit snugly between dowel 1 and the lower edge of the middle horizontal beam. Now drill holes for nailing dowel 2 to position B (to be nailed in place later).

Step 9: Drill holes in the wooden blocks and then use No. 8 box nails to nail the blocks in position C just above the notches.

Step 10: Sand all the surfaces smooth.

Step 11: Put blocks B (one on each side) below the lower horizontal beam and blocks A above the lower horizontal beam. Insert wedges about an inch into the space between block A and the upper edge of the lower horizontal beam. The lower horizontal beam should now be level and parallel to the middle beam. The loom is ready for winding. Recheck distances between dowel 2 and the middle beam and between the lower horizontal beam and the middle beam across the width of the loom. Record these distances for future reference when you reestablish warp tension.

Step 12: When winding the loom, start the warping 4 inches inside the vertical beam and end the warps about 4 inches inside the vertical beam on the other side. This leaves room for the jack and for manipulation of the wedges. It also limits the width of a rug that can be made on this loom.

Tabriz loom with movable upper beam (Loom 2)

The second type of Tabriz loom has a movable upper beam, which offers certain advantages, including ease of operation. The warp tension is established and maintained by tightening the nuts on the threaded rods, thus elevating the upper beam and tightening the warps. This is less cumbersome than the wedge arrangement used in loom 1. It has the added advantage of requiring only two inches of clearance inside the vertical beams on either side, thus a wider rug can be made than on the first loom.

A disadvantage is that it requires more sophisticated tools and equipment to build. The hole drilled in the upper horizontal movable beam must be exactly at right angles to the beam and through the very center of the beam. This can only be done with a drill press. Metal plates ⅛-inch thick must be placed on this loom in two locations: one where each threaded bolt exits through the top wooden cap that spans the space between the tops of the vertical beams, and the second plate underneath the movable upper horizontal beam where each threaded rod exits below this beam. The plate below the movable upper horizontal beam must not only be perforated but the hole must be threaded to prevent the rod from slipping out.

Loom parts. The basic parts of the loom are the same as the Tabriz loom with the movable lower beam (loom 1) with the following exceptions: (1) The slots for the movable beam are in the upper part of the vertical beams. (2) A top wooden cap (2 x 6) is required, along with the metal plates described above. (3) Bolts instead of wedges are used to increase warp tension.

Materials for loom 2 (figs. 9 and 10). Same as for loom 1 plus:

One 4-foot pine 2 x 6 for top cap
One 36-inch threaded steel rod, ½ inch in diameter

One 1 x 12 x ⅛-inch steel plate
Four nuts for ½-inch steel rod
Four additional 4-inch #12 screws for top cap
Tap and tap wrench for ½-inch hole
Ten ½-inch wood screws for metal plates

Assembly instructions. Tabriz loom 2 is constructed in the following manner:

Step 1: Cut the vertical beams, the top wooden cap, and the upper, middle, and lower horizontal beams as indicated in figures 9 and 10. Place a mark on the upper horizontal beam at a point where it will join the inside of the vertical beams when it is inserted into the slot. Drill a ¾-inch hole through the upper beam at a point centered 2 inches inside the junction of the horizontal and vertical beams on the right and left.

Step 2: Cut a slot for the movable upper horizontal beam using a power saw. Also cut slots for the fixed middle and lower horizontal beams. Cut notches in vertical beams below position C as shown.

Step 3: Notch the upper wooden cap as indicated.

Step 4: Cut the legs and braces as shown in the plans.

Step 5: Cut wooden blocks and nail them in place in position C (No. 10 box nails). (See fig. 9.)

Step 6: Cut dowels 1 and 2 so that they are as wide as the outside dimensions of the loom. Refer to figure 9 and you will see that dowel 1 is nailed in position A and dowel 2 in position B. Four 1 x 3 x ⅛-inch metal plates are needed where the threaded steel rods go through the top wooden cap and through the movable upper horizontal beam. Chisel out a seat for these four plates, which are to be placed below the hole in the movable upper horizontal beam and on top of the upper wooden cap, over the hole. Drill ½-inch holes in the top metal plates for insertion of the ½-inch threaded steel rod. Buy a ½-inch tap and tap wrench at a hardware store. On the tap and tap wrench box it tells how much smaller than ½ inch you should drill the hole you want to thread. Drill the hole in the lower plates according to that specification, and then thread the holes in the plates that go under the movable upper horizontal beam.

Step 7: Insert the upper horizontal beam into the slot so that the ends are flush with the outer surface of the vertical beams on either side.

Step 8: Insert the middle and lower stationary beams into their slots and drill holes through the back of the vertical beams in two places behind each slot for insertion of 4-inch No. 12 screws. Insert the screws through the back of the vertical beams to secure the middle and lower fixed beams in place.

---

9. *Tabriz loom 2 with movable upper beam, side view*

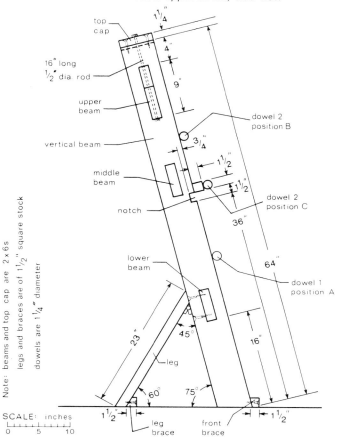

10. *Tabriz loom 2 with movable upper beam, front view*

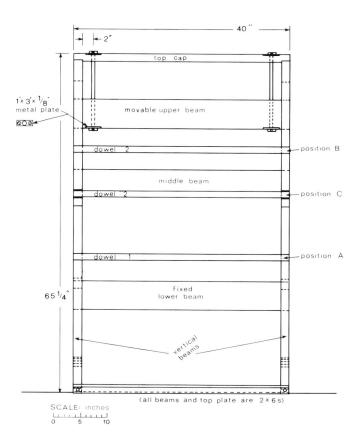

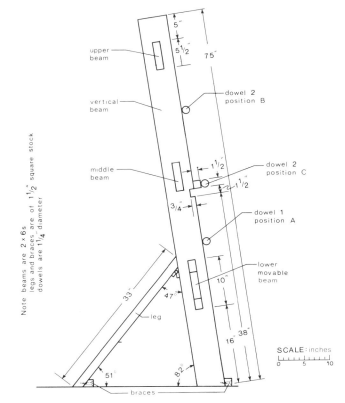

11. *Oversize Tabriz loom 3 with movable lower beam, side view*

Step 9: Use 2-inch No. 10 screws to attach the legs to the back of the vertical beams as noted in the plan, and use either chains or hinged braces to prevent overextension of the legs.

Step 10: Use No. 10 box nails to nail dowel 1 in place in position A.

Step 11: Nail dowel 2 in position B (No. 10 box nails).

Step 12: Cut two ½-inch thread steel rods 17 inches long. Insert threaded steel rods through the holes in the wooden cap and through the holes in the upper movable horizontal beam. Screw the self-locking nuts on the threaded rod below the upper horizontal beam and on the threaded rod above the wooden cap. The threaded rods will need to be replaced if the threads strip after prolonged use.

Step 13: Place 2-inch blocks in the slot above the movable horizontal beam on the right and left and tighten the nuts on the threaded rods to secure the upper beam snugly against the 2-inch blocks.

Step 14: Measure the distance between the middle beam and the upper horizontal beam to be sure the two are parallel.

Step 15: Cut out spacer S as shown in figure 8.

Oversize looms for larger rugs
(Looms 3 and 4)

When you become a hard-core weaver, you may wish to undertake the Talish rug, which takes a year and a half to complete (working forty hours a month). This rug can be woven on a smaller loom by making the knot density greater. But it seems a shame to spend that long and not have a larger rug. For this reason I am including the plans for a loom (loom 3) that make it possible to make a rug 47 inches wide. Front and side views of this loom, which has a movable lower beam, are shown in figures 11 and 12. You will need to make the loom 58 inches wide (outside width) in order to make a rug 47 inches wide. You could also adapt this loom to use a movable upper beam and a fixed lower beam, in which case the vertical beams would need to be topped with a 2 x 6-inch wooden cap for insertion of the threaded rod. In such a loom (loom 4) the upper slot would need to be 10 inches high. Both modifications are shown in figures 13 and 14. If the loom is made 58 inches wide and the upper movable beam is used, you will be able to make a rug 51 inches wide. (To construct looms 3 and 4, follow the directions for looms 1 and 2, respectively.)

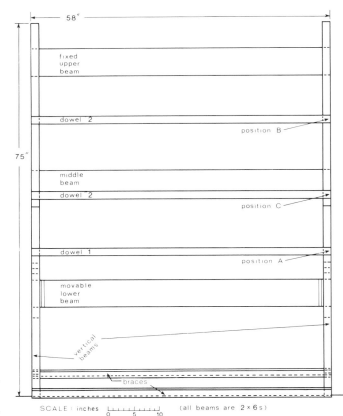

12. *Oversize Tabriz loom 3 with movable lower beam, front view*

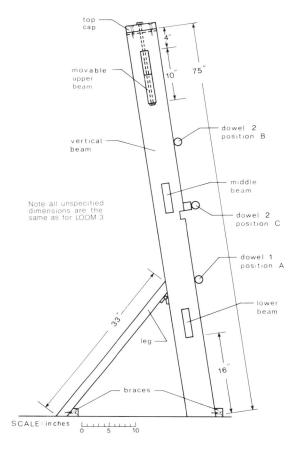

13. *Oversize Tabriz loom 4 with movable upper beam, side view*

Materials for loom 3 (figs. 11 and 12).

Two 8-foot pine 2 x 6s
Three 6-foot pine 2 x 6s
Two 5-foot pine 2 x 2s
One 6-foot pine 2 x 2 (make blocks for position C from
    scrap 2 x 2)
Nails, screws, dowels, blocks, wedges, lathe, and hinges
    as for loom 1

Materials for loom 4 (figs. 13 and 14). Same as loom 3 plus:

One 5-foot 2 x 6 for top cap
One 36-inch threaded steel rod, ½ inch in diameter
One 1 x 12 x ⅛-inch steel plate
Four nuts for ½-inch steel rod
Four additional 4-inch #12 screws for top cap
Tap and tap wrench for ½-inch hole
Ten ½-inch wood screws for metal plates

Tools

Over the past eight years I have been able to obtain tools in the United States for the construction of knotted pile rugs. This was not an easy task. I learned of American-made rug scissors from Harry Jamharian, a rug dealer and repairman. An Iranian student who worked in a rug store told me of the LeClerc weighted rug comb or beater. I found an umbrella swift in a wool shop. Finally Asghar Pahlevan's family mailed tools from Iran for construction of the finer rugs that I have made. Below are listed the tools needed and the suggested sources of supply. A supply list is found in "Sources" at the back of the book.

Umbrella swift (LeClerc #6-35-02). The Swedish umbrella swift (fig. 15) is not essential but certainly facilitates weaving. The yarn for knotted pile rugs must be made up in small skeins that are wound off larger ones. A good quality umbrella swift costs about $35. By the time your mate sits for a few hours holding the skein for you to unwind, I promise that he or she will buy you a Swedish umbrella swift and consider it a bargain. This great innovation attaches to any tabletop.

Rug comb or beater. This tool is needed to beat down the knots so that the leading edge of the rug remains straight and level. A weighted wooden rug comb (fig. 16) is made by

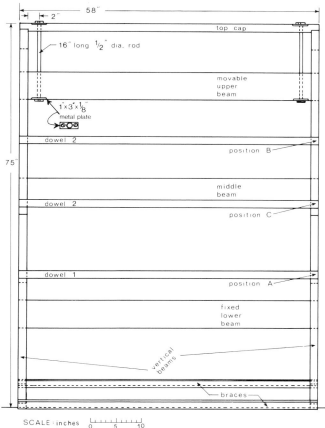

14. *Oversize Tabriz loom 4 with movable upper beam, front view*

LeClerc in Canada (#6-15-35). Because of the lead weight in the handle, this implement is quite adequate for rugs of up to ten knots per horizontal inch.

For rugs finer than ten knots per inch you will need a Middle Eastern metal daftoon (fig. 17) or rug beater. For suggestions on how to obtain a daftoon, see the ''Sources'' chapter.

Shuttle. Also needed is a flat wooden shuttle (fig. 18) for passing the weft.

Knife. A 4- to 5-inch paring knife is good for cutting the yarn after you tie the knots (fig. 19). It needs to be sharpened periodically.

Hook. A No. 7 crochet hook is used in rug construction and is particularly useful for correcting mistakes in the previous row and for splicing broken warp thread.

Scissors. Excellent German-angled scissors with a wide lower blade (fig. 20) can be obtained in the United States (WASA 32-nic from Soligner, Germany). Wiss U.S.A. makes a satisfactory rug scissors (RS-1), but the narrow lower blade is a disadvantage (fig. 21). Either scissors is satisfactory for cutting the rows of pile, but they are not quite as good as rug scissors that can be obtained from Iran or Turkey (fig. 22).

Thimble. A leather thimble (fig. 23) protects your right index fingertip and prevents your fingernail from being notched by pulling down on the knots.

Materials for warp, weft, and pile

Warps in Oriental rugs are made of wool, cotton, or silk. Silk warp is used in very fine Iranian rugs from Isfahan, Nain, and Tabriz and in some Turkoman rugs. It is not available in the United States. Woolen warp is used in many tribal rugs because it is readily available. Wool has some drawbacks, as will be discussed in Chapter 2. The main reason I use it is that it makes a replica of a tribal rug look more authentic.

15. Umbrella swift (LeClerc #6-35-02)

Before I go into the detailed relationships of *woolen* warp and weft material, I suggest that you refer to Table 1. This outlines the various materials used for warp and weft and indicates the rug design in which these combinations are used.

Warp material. A good brand of woolen warp available in the United States is Navajo warp. It is a strong three-ply

Table 1: Woolen Warp, Weft, and Knot Combinations

| | Knots per Vertical Inch | |
	13	10
Pile material	7/2 wool doubled	7/2 wool doubled
Woolen warp	Navajo warp, 7 pairs per horizontal inch	Navajo warp, 7 pairs per horizontal inch
Loose weft	7/2 wool single	Navajo warp
Weft under tension	Navajo warp	Navajo warp
Rug design	Turkoman (Design 7)	Qashgai duck rug (Design 6) Albuturkey rug (Design 3)

16. *The weighted wooden comb is used for compacting rows of knots.*

17. *Iranian daftoon (weighted metal comb)*

18. *The shuttle is used for passing weft.*

19. *Paring knife*

20. *WASA rug scissors (32-nic)*

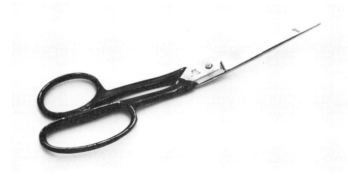

21. *Wiss rug scissors (RS-1)*

22. *Iranian rug scissors*

23. Leather thimble

ply but of a finer caliber than the 12 series. The 12/6 can be used to achieve ten to fourteen warp pairs per horizontal inch and 12/9 for seven to eight warp pairs per horizontal inch. The 30/9 is used for weft.

Woolen weft. The choice of weft material partly determines the number of rows of knots per vertical inch. In the rugs with woolen warp, I use woolen weft. All the woolen warp rug designs in this book have seven pairs of warps per horizontal inch. If you use the Navajo warp as the weft under tension, the 7/2 wool as the loose sinuous weft, and doubled 7/2 wool for the knots, you get thirteen knots per vertical inch. If you use Navajo warp for the sinuous loose weft, Navajo warp as the weft under tension, and doubled 7/2 wool for knots, you get nine or ten knots per vertical inch.

woolen warp and is quite satisfactory for use in rugs with up to seven warp pairs per horizontal inch. It has little tendency to fray or break under tension.

Table 2 shows the cotton warp/weft relationship. Keep in mind that the number of knots per vertical inch may vary (from eight to ten, for example) depending on the amount of tension on the warps. You should monitor the knots per vertical inch and adjust the tension to get the desired number (more tension results in better compacting and more knots per vertical inch).

The best cotton warp I have found is a tightly spun Egyptian cotton called fishnet twine. The three sizes of fishnet twine that I use are 12/6, 12/9, and 30/9. The cotton fibers of the 12 series are the same size, but the finer of the two, 12/6, is six-ply and the other is nine-ply. The 30/9 is nine-

Cotton weft. It comes as no surprise that you use cotton warp with cotton weft. Before going further please refer to Table 2. The 16/2 cotton doubled makes good sinuous weft material, since it is loosely spun and limp. The 16/2 cotton doubled and used as the loose weft, with 1.5 millimeter Haitian cotton as taut weft and fourteen pairs of 12/6 fishnet twine warps per inch, and with 7/2 single strand for knots, yields thirteen rows of knots per vertical inch.

The 12/6 fishnet twine can also be used as ten pairs of warps per horizontal inch. Use 12/6 fishnet twine as the weft under tension and also 12/6 fishnet twine as the loose sinuous weft to obtain ten knots per vertical inch. With this combination, of course, 7/2 wool doubled is used for knots.

The 12/9 fishnet twine can be used as seven or eight pairs of warps per horizontal inch. If you use 7/2 wool dou-

Table 2: Cotton Warp, Weft, and Knot Combinations

| | Knots per Vertical Inch | | | | |
	9*	8	10	13	12.5
Pile material	7/2 wool doubled	7/2 wool doubled	7/2 wool doubled	7/2 wool single	7/2 wool doubled
Cotton warp	12/9 fishnet twine, 7 pairs per horizontal inch	12/9 fishnet twine, 8 pairs per horizontal inch	12/6 fishnet twine, 10 pairs per horizontal inch	12/6 fishnet twine, 14 pairs per horizontal inch	12/9 fishnet twine, 8 pairs per horizontal inch
Loose weft	12/9 fishnet twine	12/9 fishnet twine	12/6 fishnet twine	16/2 cotton doubled	30/9 fishnet twine
Weft under tension	12/9 fishnet twine	12/9 fishnet twine	12/6 fishnet twine	1.5 mm Haitian or other loosely spun 1.5 mm cotton	30/9 fishnet twine
Rug design	Shiraz mat (Design 1)	Chinese rug (Design 5) Shiraz mat (Design 4)	Talish rug (Design 8) Gendje mat (Design 2)	Kashan rug (Design 9)	Turkoman rug (Design 7)

* When you use 7 warp pairs per horizontal inch, the knots compact and flatten, so you get 9 per vertical inch. The number of knots per square inch is about the same as in column 2, namely 64 knots per square inch.

bled for knots and 12/9 fishnet twine for both loose and taut weft, and 12/9 fishnet twine for warps, seven pairs per horizontal inch, you get nine knots per vertical inch. If you use 7/2 wool doubled for knots and 12/9 fishnet twine for both loose and taut weft and 12/9 fishnet twine for warps, eight pairs per horizontal inch, you get eight knots per vertical inch. The 12/9 with eight warp pairs per inch can be used with 30/9 fishnet twine as both taut and loose weft to get 12.5 knots per vertical inch. The 7/2 wool doubled is used for knots.

The warp/weft relationships listed in the tables are the ones needed for making the rug designs presented in this book. Warp and weft of any other diameter will distort the designs. As you copy other rugs, you will encounter other warp/weft relationships. At that point you will have to make samples and try different materials until the warp/weft relationship approximates that in the rug you are copying.

Pile material. The wool for pile comes from three sources:

1. Scandinavian 7/2 wool (tuna garn) is used for the pile in all of the rug designs in Chapter 5. This is the ideal wool for Oriental rugs and most closely approximates the wool of the finer rugs of the Middle East. Cheaper American yarn gives the rug a softer undesirable texture, wears poorly, and is often slightly thicker, so that the design is distorted.

2. Harrisville two-ply yarn, an American product, is cheaper than the Scandinavian yarn, but it is slightly harsher and also slightly thicker in caliber. Used as a minor color in a rug made predominantly with the Scandinavian yarn, it will not distort the design. Harrisville cream beige is an especially nice color.

3. Three-ply Paterna Persian yarn is quite expensive, but does offer subtle gradations of reds and other colors so necessary in some of the finer Oriental rugs. It can be mixed with the other yarns mentioned and is especially useful when you need, for example, three or more shades of red.

Obtaining materials. If you adhere to the following general advice, you will avoid some of the problems that I have encountered in obtaining materials.

The Scandinavian wool (tuna garn) is perfect for knotted pile weaving and gives the rug the texture of a fine-quality Oriental rug. Unfortunately, this wool is not widely used by American craftsmen and few wool stores stock it.

I have found it complicated to order directly from an overseas supplier. It may take two months or more to get an order filled. (Please refer to "Sources" at the back of the book.)

It is critical that you use the various sizes of fishnet twine for warp and weft. If you use a substitute of a slightly different caliber or strength, the results will probably cause you to abandon a hobby that would otherwise give you a great deal of pleasure.

The tools are less of a problem to obtain than the woolen and cotton materials. They are made in Canada and the United States.

Further suggestions on suppliers, along with their addresses, are found in "Sources."

How to estimate yarn needs. You can calculate the approximate length of warp needed for the loom by measuring the distance from the top horizontal beam to the bottom beam and around and back up to the top beam. Then multiply this distance by the number of warps and multiply that product by two. This gives you the length of warp needed.

Detailed information on warp, weft, and pile is given with each design in Chapter 5. You have to guess at the amount needed for each color of wool by estimating the rough percentage of the various colors. If you have wool left over, it can be used for another rug. Also, wool shops will exchange wool if the skein has not been opened.

In rugs of from 60 to 100 knots per inch use 7/2 woolen two-ply yarn doubled for pile. In finer rugs, such as the Kashan shown in plate I (180 knots per square inch), two-ply 7/2 wool is used.

For pile, if you use 7/2 wool doubled, you will need about one skein of yarn for every 2,500 knots. If you use 7/2 wool two-ply for pile, you will need about one skein for every 5,000 knots.

CHAPTER 2

General Considerations

If you are to make an Oriental rug, several basic principles must be mastered. You must string a loom with warp threads that can be separated into two sheds. The warps must be spaced with the desired number per inch and uniform tension maintained during weaving. You will weave a heading at the beginning and at the end of the rug, and you will bind the sides of the rug with selvage. The rug will consist of rows of either Ghiordes or Senna knots, with usually two rows of weft between each two rows of knots. The tension on the warps and the method of inserting the weft greatly affect the shape of the rug and the uniformity of the design.

This may sound complicated at first, but if you deal with each of these principles individually, rug construction becomes logical and easily understood. First you must warp the loom.

Preparing the loom for warping

Block the movable beam. Place block B in the slot below the movable lower beam so that the beam will remain stationary during warping (fig. 24). Place block A and the wedge above the lower beam in the slot to immobilize the lower beam. The block and wedge must be of the same dimensions on both right and left sides, so that the lower beam is equidistant from the middle beam along its entire length. The wedge must be inserted only about one inch, so that the tension on the warps can be increased after warping. If the loom with the movable upper beam is used, a 2-inch block should be placed in the slots above the upper beam and the threaded rods used to tighten the beam against the blocks.

Nail dowels in place. Use No. 10 box nails to nail dowel 1 to the front of the loom in position A, which is 4 inches above the top of the lower horizontal beam (fig. 25). If spacer S is used, the dowel is nailed so that the spacer fits between dowel 1 and the middle beam. This allows room for your hand and the spool of warp thread to encircle dowel 1 during the warping process. Nail dowel 2 in position B, which is about midway between the upper and center beams.

Prevent bending of dowel 1. Place spacer between dowel 1 and center beam (fig. 25). If spacer is not used, tie soft, heavy twine around dowel 1 and the lower beam to prevent bowing of dowel 1 during warping.

Check measurements. Check all measurements before beginning the warping procedure. The lower beam and dowel 1 must be parallel to the center beam. The lower beam and the dowel must be equidistant from the center beams throughout their length.

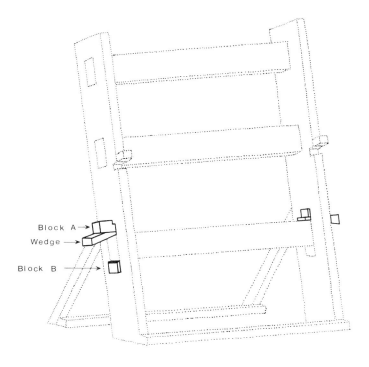

Block A
Wedge
Block B

24. Use blocks and wedges to immobilize the lower beam in preparation for warping.

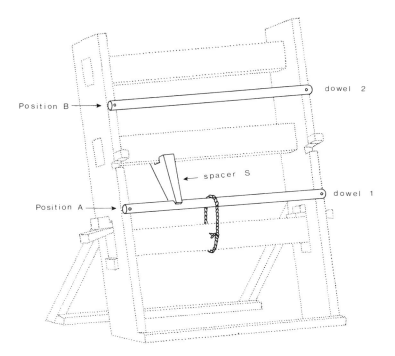

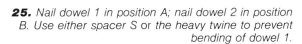

25. Nail dowel 1 in position A; nail dowel 2 in position B. Use either spacer S or the heavy twine to prevent bending of dowel 1.

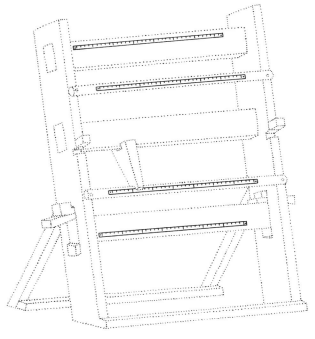

26. Secure the tape measures with glue to the top and bottom beams and to dowels 1 and 2.

Apply tape measures to loom. Finally, place a tape measure of appropriate length on the upper horizontal beam, the lower horizontal beam, dowel 1, and dowel 2 (fig. 26). All these tape measures must begin 4 inches inside the left vertical beam and end 4 inches to the left of the right vertical beam. They are directly one above the other to guide you in stringing the warp thread. If the loom with the movable upper beam is used (loom 2), the tapes may begin and end 2 inches inside the vertical beams, making possible a wider rug.

The warping process

Step 1: To dowel 1 tie warp thread 4 inches (or 2 inches if the loom with a movable upper beam, loom 2, is used) inside the left vertical beam. (See fig. 27.) Use warp thread of the type indicated in the design. If you use loom 2 and need to continue warping within 2 inches of the right vertical beam, you must reserve a spool of warp 2 inches or less in diameter. You will be able to wind the last few inches of warp without being cramped for space. If you are left-handed, you may find it easier to wind the warp starting from the right and proceeding to the left.

Step 2: Hold the spool of warp in the right palm (or left palm if you are left-handed) and let the string exit between the second and third fingers. This allows you to keep the warp under tension.

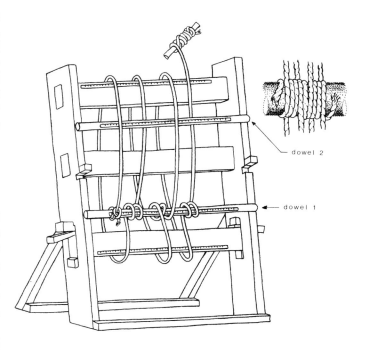

27. The warping process begins. Note warp goes alternately in front and in back of dowel 2. Insert shows encircling threads packed together to act as spacers.

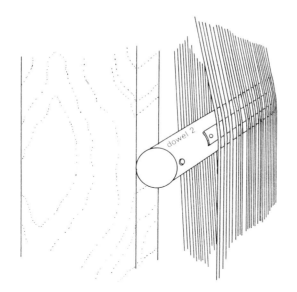

Step 3: Direct the warp thread in front of dowel 2, over the top horizontal beam, down behind the loom, underneath the lower horizontal beam, and behind dowel 1, immediately to the right of the beginning of the warp thread (fig. 27).

Step 4: Maintaining tension, encircle dowel 1 two times from back to front and pack down the encircling threads tightly with a fingernail.

Step 5: As the second encircling turn is wound and packed down, direct the warp thread from behind dowel 1 to a position behind dowel 2.

Step 6: Bring the warp thread over the top of the top horizontal beam, downward behind the loom, around the lower horizontal beam, and back to dowel 1. (Tension must be constantly maintained during this procedure.)

Step 7: On this round, go in front of dowel 1, encircle it two times, pack the encircling threads together, and direct the warp in front of dowel 2. Then go over the upper horizontal

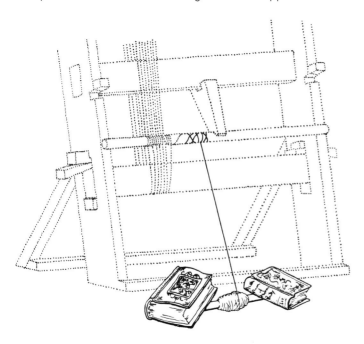

28. *The front and back warps are separated by dowel 2 for later shed formation.*

beam, down the back of the loom and under the lower beam, and back to dowel 1 again. This time the warp goes behind dowel 1 and encircles it twice, and then goes behind dowel 2, etc. (fig. 27 and insert).

The encircling of dowel 1 and the packing of the threads together result in evenly spaced warp threads. For example, when using 12/9 fishnet twine, the spacing of two encircling threads between each continuing thread gives you seven pairs of threads per inch: seven in front and seven in back of dowel 2. When 12/6 fishnet twine is used, the spacing is ten pairs per inch with two encircling threads between each continuing thread. If you use Navajo warp, encircle dowel 1 twice, and pack the threads together, you get seven warp pairs per inch. A constant monitoring of this spacing can be done by reference to the tape measures nailed on the dowels and the upper and lower beams. In some instances, you may not need to pack the encircling threads together but may, for example, just encircle the dowel one time and depend on reference to the tape measure to give you eight, ten, or even fourteen pairs of front and back threads per inch. Only encircle dowel 1 one time when using 12/9 warp, eight per inch, or 12/6 warp, fourteen per inch.

By going alternately in front of and behind dowel 1, front and back threads are separated on the front of the loom, since these threads also go alternately in front of and behind dowel 2. These threads are kept apart for later construction of two sheds (fig. 28).

Step 8: As the warping process continues, keep spacer S between dowel 1 and the middle horizontal beam. Spacer S or the encircling twine should be about 6 inches to the right of the area being warped, and will have to be moved periodically as the warping progresses. Spacer S or the encircling twine helps to prevent any bowing of dowel 1 that would result from the tension of the warp threads being wound.

Step 9: The phone usually rings in the middle of the warping process. If you must interrupt the process, wrap the ball of twine four or five times around dowel 1 and place books over either end of the spool to maintain tension. This prevents any slack from developing in the warp (fig. 29).

Step 10: When one spool of warp thread is depleted, tie it to dowel 1 while maintaining tension. Then tie the end of a new spool of warp thread to dowel 1, overlapping the last tie, and continue warping. It is a good idea to look periodically at the warp from the side to make sure you have not mistakenly gone behind dowel 2 when you should have gone in front of it. If you have, there will be warp thread going diagonally across the space between the front and back warp threads

29. *Secure the spool of twine under two books to allow interruption of warping without losing tension.*

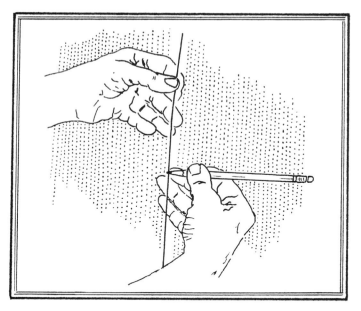

30. *It is helpful to mark every tenth warp with a pencil to facilitate a tally during warping.*

instead of the nice wedge-shaped shed that should be developing. The warping is carried out to within 4 inches (or 2 inches if using a movable upper horizontal beam) of the right vertical beam. Of course, the number of warp threads needed for the rug was previously calculated, and the warp threads should be counted periodically to tell when the proper number has been reached. It is sometimes helpful to mark every tenth front warp thread with a pencil so that you do not have to start the counting from the first of the threads each time you stop for a tally (fig. 30).

Preparing the loom for tying heddles

Now take the nails out of dowel 2 and pull it down to about the level of the middle beam (fig. 31A).

Round off the end of dowel 3 and place it between the front and back warp strings, midway between dowel 2 and the top horizontal beam (fig. 31B). Dowel 3 should be suspended from the upper horizontal beam by two strings. This prevents it from coming out accidentally. If that were to happen, the loom would either have to be rewarped or the front and back threads separated somehow.

Slide dowel 2 out from between the warp threads (fig. 31C). Now dowel 3 separates the front and back warps.

31. *(A) Remove the nails from dowel 2 and move it to a position just above blocks in position C. (B) Insert dowel 3 between the front and back warps and suspend the dowel as shown. (C) Remove dowel 2. (D) Nail dowel 2 to its new position on the front of wooden blocks in position C.*

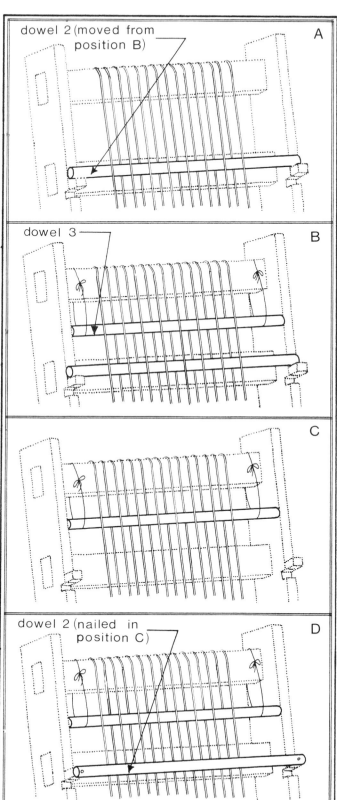

dowel 2 (moved from position B) — A

dowel 3 — B

C

dowel 2 (nailed in position C) — D

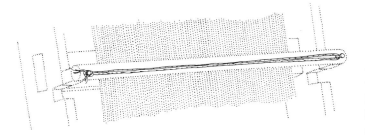

Use No. 20 finishing nails to renail dowel 2 to its new position on the blocks at the front of the vertical beams in position C (fig. 31D). This is done in preparation for tying the heddles around the back warp threads. Leave about ⅛ inch of the head of the nails protruding above the surface of dowel 2, to attach a string as noted below.

Tie a length of warp thread around the protruding nail on the left side of dowel 2, stretch it across tightly around the nail on the right side of dowel 2, and take it back to its origin and tie it tightly. This results in a doubled thickness of warp thread across the front surface of dowel 2 (fig. 32).

Tying the heddles

Step 1: Place dowel 3 against the bottom edge of the top horizontal beam. (Tie in position if necessary.)

Step 2: Make a small skein with 5 or 6 feet of the warp thread by winding it around an outstretched thumb and fore-finger and secure this with a small, loosely tied piece of string so that it will not get tangled but will unravel easily.

Step 3: Tie this string to the string stretched across the front of dowel 2 at a position just to the left of the first front warp thread, left side.

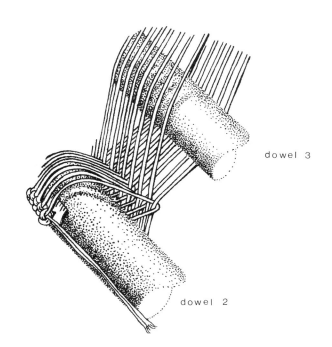

dowel 3

dowel 2

32. *Tie a doubled warp thread between the nails in dowel 2.*

Step 4: The skein of string is then directed above dowel 2 to the left of the first front warp and goes behind the first back warp, encircling it and pulling it forward (fig. 33).

Step 5: Then it comes below dowel 2 and is tied to the string stretched across dowel 2 with a single simple knot. This knot has to be tied with tension that will angle the back warp thread to a position about ¼ inch behind the front warp thread (fig. 33). Thus, the back warp thread is pulled forward in a V shape with the apex of the V just behind the front warp thread. (Heddles are tied for *all* warp pairs, including selvage pairs.)

Step 6: After tying the single knot, direct the skein be-tween the first and second front warps. It then goes behind the second back warp thread, and pulls it forward as the skein is pulled below dowel 2 and once again tied to the string stretched across dowel 2. Tie this so that the back warp thread is angled to a position where it is about ¼ inch behind the front warp thread.

Step 7: The single knots can be packed together along the string on the front of dowel 2 so that the threads that go be-tween the front strings to pick up the back strings go at a 90-degree angle to dowel 2 (fig. 33).

Step 8: After a few of the back threads have been tied for-ward, it is good to examine the sheds to see if the threads are in the proper position. This is done as follows. Pull dowel 3 down to a position just above the heddles. In this position there should be a space of about ⅜ inch between the front and back warp threads, with the front threads in front and the back threads in back. *This relationship is shed #1* (fig. 34). If such a space is not available for passage of the shut-tle, it is likely that the back warp threads have been pulled too far forward. In that case, the heddles must be redone and loosened slightly so that when dowel 3 is in the lower position (just above the heddles), a shuttle can be passed easily between the front and back warp threads, with the front threads in front and the back threads in back. *Shed #2 is in position when dowel 3 is placed as high as it will go just below the bottom of the top horizontal beam* (fig. 35). With the dowel in that position, press on the front threads about 6 inches above the heddles with your forearm; this pushes the front threads backward. At this point, shed #2 is created with the back threads in front and the front threads in back.

Step 9: Even though both sheds are accessible after you tie the heddles, later in rug construction either shed #1 or shed #2 may decrease in depth, and shuttle insertion may be difficult. This is likely to occur when the rug is moved to the back of the loom and the leading edge of the weaving is at the top of the lower horizontal beam. In this situation you

33. *The heddles hold the back warps to a position about ¼ inch behind the front warps.*

SHED #1

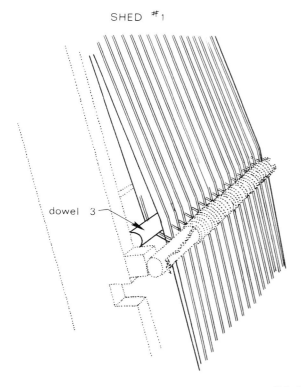

dowel 3

34. *Shed #1*

SHED #2

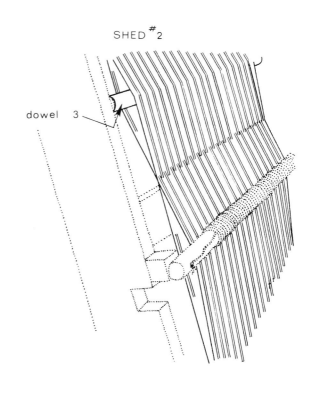

dowel 3

35. *Shed #2*

may remove the nails in dowel 2 and change the thickness of the blocks under the dowel. A thicker block will increase the depth of shed #2; a thinner block will increase the depth of shed #1. Of course, for this maneuver you will need to cut loose from the nails the string stretched across dowel 2. But the series of single knots will not be disturbed by cutting this string.

Step 10: Pack the series of single knots together so that they make a beaded appearance on the string stretched on the front of dowel 2 (fig. 36). Continue the process until all the back warp threads are pulled forward by the heddles. The thread for the heddles must be knotted periodically. The small skein of thread for the heddle tends to become tangled at times, but with patience it will untangle and the heddling process can be completed.

When the process is completed, the last warp on the right side should be a front one. Go through the warp strings a pair at a time to make sure that none of the back threads have been skipped. It is not a bad idea to do this periodically as the heddling procedure is done. You can readily see that if some of the back warp threads are missed, some of the pairs of threads will be unequal with one front thread and two back threads. This is not a tragedy, because in the weaving process the extraneous back warp thread can merely be left

out of the rug, but it is much nicer if all the front threads are perfectly matched with the back threads. When you check the shed, if you find that in one or two places some of the back threads are not pulled as far forward as the other back warp threads, this can be corrected by individual heddles, which are tied around the string, pulling it forward to a proper position. If this is not done, the shuttle will go on the wrong side of the back threads at times and will leave exposed warp thread showing on the back of the rug. After the warping procedure is completed, you are ready to start the weaving process. This is dealt with in the next chapter.

Maintaining tension

American weavers are not accustomed to weaving on warps as tense as one needs for knotted pile weaving. The warps are strung on the loom under tension. After warping, the tension is increased even more by one of two methods. Two looms are pictured in the previous chapter. The one

36. *As you secure the heddles with knots, the knots will have a beaded appearance.*

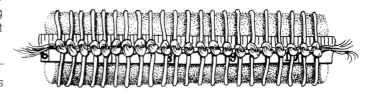

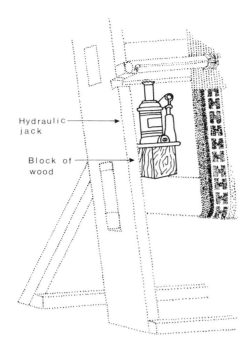

with the movable lower beam (loom 1) increases tension by driving wedges in between the upper limit of the slot in the vertical beam and the upper portion of the lower horizontal beam (figs. 6 and 7). As the wedges are driven in, they force the lower beam downward. The second method (loom 2, figs. 9 and 10) involves a movable upper beam. Tension is increased on the warps in this type of loom by tightening the threaded bolts, thrusting the upper beam upward, and increasing tension on the warps. Whichever method is used, the tension is increased until the warps can be strummed like guitar strings.

With the proper tension you can press on the warps with the flat of your hand without pushing the strings backward much. This degree of tension is usually obtained when the lower or upper beam, as the case may be, is displaced up to about half an inch in the direction of increasing tension, depending on the tightness of the warps and the elasticity of the warp material. This is after the strings are already taut from being wound on the loom. To give you some idea of how tight the strings must be, I originally made my looms out of 2 x 4s. A loom 4½ feet wide was constructed. After I had warped the loom and increased the tension on the strings to the proper degree for weaving, I noted that the upper beam was warped downward in a curved fashion about a half inch just by the tension of the warps.

I have had the most experience with the loom having the movable lower beam and wedges for production of tension (loom 1). In my earlier experience I found it difficult to insert the wedge. I tried using a wedge that was quite thin at the entering end, but it was made of softwood and splintered after multiple removals and reinsertions. So I converted to wedges made of hardwood. This solved the splintering problem, but it was still difficult to insert the wedges into the loom. The problem was intensified when I reached the point

of moving the rug to the back of the loom. After moving the rug to the back, it was easy enough to insert the first block and wedge on the right side of the loom, but on the left side there was scarcely room for the block, and the wedge could be inserted easily only if I found some method of forcefully pressing the lower beam downward on the left side. I found that a good solution is a small hydraulic jack. It can be placed on a 4 x 4 x 6-inch block of wood resting on the lower beam (fig. 37). As the jack is raised, it engages the middle beam and forces the lower beam downward. Then the wedge and block on the left side can easily be placed and the jack removed (fig. 38). The wedge is driven in the necessary distance to make the lower beam parallel to the middle beam.

Problem of unequal tension. Something inherent in winding the warp from left to right often results in the warps on the right half of the loom being tighter than those on the left half, even though the lower beam ends are equidistant from the middle beam and an effort is made to maintain even tension on the warp as it is wound. By the time two or three inches of the rug are woven, any inequality in the tension will be apparent. The rows of knots pack down more compactly on the side where the *warps are under the greater tension.* Often the left side of the rug will be one-fourth inch higher in the vertical dimension than the right side of the rug by the time three inches of rug are woven. If

38. *Insert the wedge and block A and remove jack.*

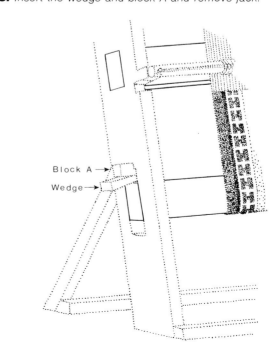

39. *Insert loose weft from right to left and form equal bubbles.*

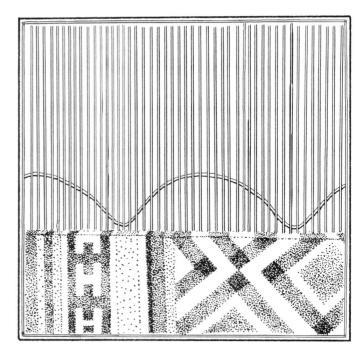

this is not corrected, a three-foot rug will end up three inches longer on the left side than on the right. One sees such irregularities in Oriental rugs. It is "no big deal" in the Middle East, where hardly anything is perfectly square, including rooms, doors, picture frames, or gardens. But the rugs woven by experts are usually nearly square and symmetrical, and that should be our goal. So by the time you see an increase of one-eighth inch in length on one side of the rug (usually the left side), drive the wedge in enough to equalize the tension on the warps. Often this requires up to a half inch greater depression of the lower beam on the side of the lesser tension.

Adjustments after moving the rug on the loom.
Every time the rug is moved to the back of the loom, the tension must be reestablished. This is done by driving the wedges in to recreate the same space between the middle and lower beams on the right and left sides of the loom. In this way the tension is kept constant and the designs will not vary in height from one end of the rug to the other. From the beginning to the end of the rug, the tension on the warp must be constant. It may result in the lower beam being slanted downward on one side and not parallel to the middle beam. The need for a slightly slanted movable beam is the reason why the holes for the threaded bolts in the upper beams are larger than the bolts. This allows for a slight tilt of the movable upper beam to assure uniform tension on the threads.

Keeping the width uniform

Those of you who have weaving experience need not be told how to prevent the sides of the rug from pulling in, but bear with me as I let beginning weavers (as I was initially) in on the secret.

Use of sufficient weft. It is the insertion of insufficient weft that results in the edges of the rug being pulled in. In flat weaving the problem is fairly simple: bubbles of weft must be consistent in size to assure a uniform width of the fabric. A greater length of weft in one portion of the fabric and less in another will result in a fabric with ripples: it will not lie flat in an area of too much weft and will pull in at the sides in areas of too little weft.

Problems peculiar to knotted pile weaving. Each row of knots is separated by weft. A few Persian rugs are single wefted: they have only one row of weft between each row of knots. This results in a speckled appearance on the back of the rug, because only every other warp is covered by weft on the back. The more usual arrangement in the Middle East is two rows of weft between each row of

knots. This may be done with the wefts put in from right to left without tension (fig. 39). Then the shed is reversed and the weft is placed from right to left again without tension.

A good way to put a consistent length of weft into the rug is to insert bubbles of equal width and height with each weft passage. If the bubbles of weft are too big, redundant weft will be seen between the warp threads on the back of the rug. If the bubbles of weft are too small, the weft pulls the warps together with two results: (1) the rug pulls in at the sides and gets progressively narrower, and (2) in the areas where the warps are pulled closer together there is a bulge in the leading edge of the rug (fig. 40). The idea is to put equal lengths of weft in the two sheds, giving you a knot with no depression of the warps and two wefts that are equally sinuous. This is a commonly used technique, particularly in the village rugs. For the novice weaver this weft technique is not recommended, since it will probably produce a rug that does not lie flat or that pulls in at the sides. Experienced weavers will probably have little problem with the technique, and it results in a soft and pliable rug.

A good technique for weft insertion. A common technique and, in my opinion, an easier one for the beginner is the use of one weft under tension and one weft put in without tension so that it is very sinuous.

Step 1: Two shuttles are used and both weft threads are started from the right side of the loom.
Step 2: With dowel 3 down (shed #1, front warps in front and back warps in back), the first weft is placed under slight tension and packed in place with the beater. This results in a depression of each of the pair of warps, with the degree of depression dependent on two factors—the thickness of the weft and the closeness of the warp threads to each other.

40. High and low places in the leading edge of the rug result from incorrect weft insertion.

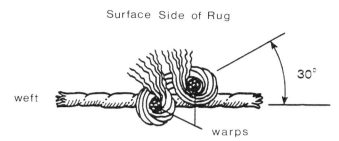

41. A moderately thick weft under tension causes a slight depression of every other warp. (Ghiordes knot)

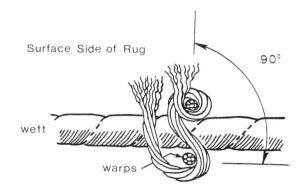

42. A still thicker weft combined with closely spaced warps results in a 90-degree depression of every other warp. (Senna knot)

With eight warp pairs per inch, for example, a weft under tension the same size as the warp thread results in about a 30-degree depression of every other warp (fig. 41). If there are fourteen pairs of warps per inch, a weft under tension three times the diameter of the warp will result in a warp depression of 90 degrees. Therefore, only one warp covered by the pile material is seen on the back of the rug for each knot (fig. 42). More about this is found in the following section about knots.

Step 3: The second weft is placed through the shed in bubbles without tension when the front warps are displaced backward and the back warps are forward.

Step 4: On coarser rugs, an alternative is to beat the looser weft in with the rug beater. Just hold a 6-inch segment of weft loosely at an angle of about 45 degrees and beat it into the warp so that the weft is sinuous (fig. 43). Increasing the angle at which you hold the weft inserts more weft, and decreasing the angle inserts less weft. On finer rugs, such as the Kashan shown in plate I, this method does not work well. Instead, you should make small bubbles with the blunt end of the crochet hook so that the weft is the proper length when you beat it down. (See fig. 66.) With one of the above methods insert the loose weft.

Knots

Two types of knots are used in most Oriental rugs: the Turkish or Ghiordes knot and the Senna knot. Techniques for tying these knots are illustrated in Chapter 3 (figs. 64 and 65).

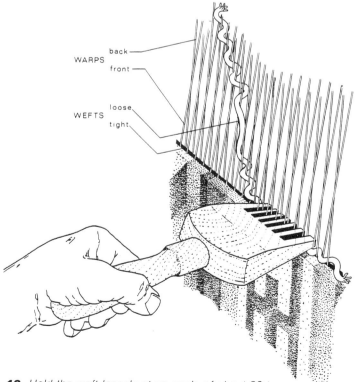

43. Hold the weft loosely at an angle of about 30 to 45 degrees, beating it in with a rug comb so that just the right amount of weft is inserted. This method is superior to the bubble method for loose weft insertion. The greater the angle, the more weft goes in.

The Senna knot. This asymmetrical knot (sometimes called Sehna or Senneh) is named after the ancient town of Senna (Sinneh), now Sanandaj. Surprisingly, the knot used in Sanandaj is not the Senna knot, but the Turkish or symmetrical knot. This is surprising to all except those who have lived in Iran, a land of paradoxes. In the four and a half years I was there, I learned that Iranian saws cut on the upstroke not the downstroke, Iranians deal cards counterclockwise, and white is the color of mourning. So I am not surprised that the Turkish knot is used in the city of origin of the Senna knot.

The Senna knot can be used in coarsely knotted rugs. In Chinese rugs it is used almost exclusively. In Iran it is most often used in finely knotted rugs with deeply depressed warps. This makes sense, for as the warps lie closer together there may be insufficient room for warps to lie side by side. The Senna knot encircles the front warp closest to the surface of the rug and depresses it 90 degrees. The pile thread then goes around the warp that one sees on the back of the rug without encircling it (figs. 44 and 45). In modern Chinese rugs for some reason the opposite situation prevails. The encircled warp is the back one and the nonencircled warp is depressed to near the surface of the rug (fig. 46). I would recommend the Senna knot for any rugs with twelve or more pairs of warps per inch. For most coarser rugs, the Turkish knot is more suitable.

If you are left-handed, you will find it easier to tie the

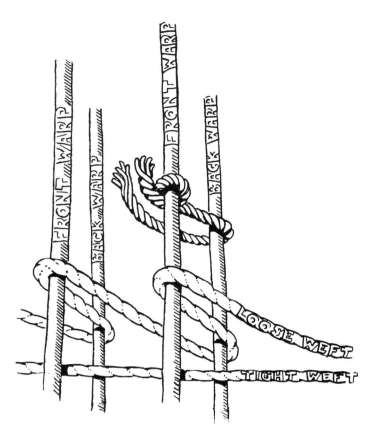

45. *A three-dimensional representation of the Senna knot*

Surface Side of Rug

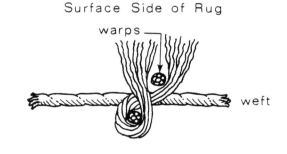

46. *Chinese Senna knot*

Senna knot by encircling the left warp of each pair. The result will be a Chinese Senna knot, open to the right. The same is true of the Ghiordes knot: a left-handed person finds it easier to tie around the left warp first.

The Turkish or Ghiordes knot. This knot encircles each of the pairs of warps and the ends come out between the warps (fig. 47). I find that the rug lies flatter and is less likely to pull in at the edges if one weft is put in under tension as described above so that every other warp is slightly depressed. This also makes for a heavier rug with a firmer body when it is folded over on itself.

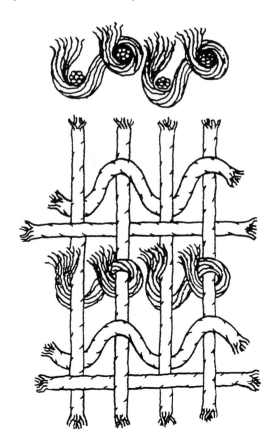

44. *The Senna knot*

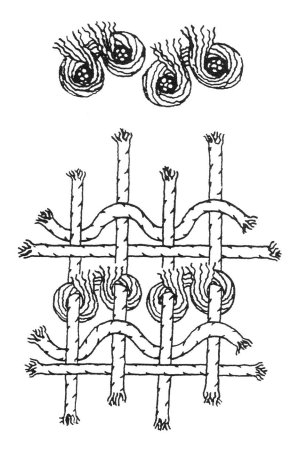

47. *Ghiordes knot*

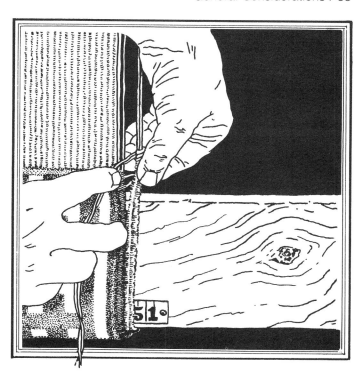

49. *If the weft is too loose as it engages the next to the last pair of warps, a gap develops between the selvage and the body of the rug.*

Selvage

The selvage is the binding for the sides of the rug. I usually start the selvage by tying a Ghiordes knot on the pair of warps three pairs from the edge of the rug (fig. 48). After each row of knots and wefts is placed, I wind the woolen four-ply selvage material, which was secured with the knot, in a figure 8 fashion five or six times around the outer two pairs of warps. The wefts do not engage the outer pair of warps on either side, so the figure 8 arrangement of the selvage unites the outer pair of warps to the rug and prevents the weft from showing on the sides of the rug (fig. 48). If the weft encircles the second warp pair from the edge too loosely, one sees a gap between the outer two pairs of warp threads and the rug when tension is placed on this selvage. You should periodically pull laterally on the selvage to see if a gap is present (fig. 49). If there is a gap, you can fix it by whipstitching the selvage to the body of the rug—use a needle threaded with 7/2 wool—or by periodically engaging the third pair of warps from the edge in the figure 8 binding (fig. 50). Such a gap is prevented by having no redundant weft where the weft encircles the second pair of warps from the edge.

Designs

As one creates the design in the rug, it is essential for the design in each row to be correct and correlated with the

48. *Bind the sides of the rug with a figure 8 wrap around the outer two pairs of warps.*

50. *The gap is repaired by wrapping selvage around the third pair of warps from the edge.*

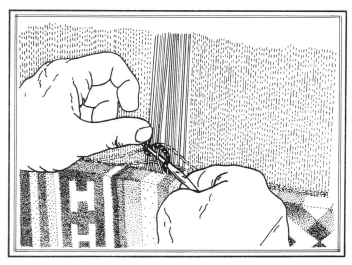

51. *A mistake in the color of a knot in the previous row can be corrected. Just loosen the weft, remove the knot and tie on the proper color with a crochet hook.*

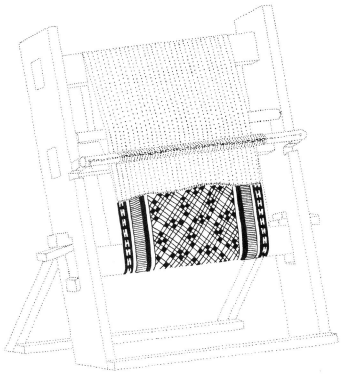

52. *Humps and depressions in the leading edge can be corrected by varying the force of beating down knots and putting in adequate weft.*

Keeping the line of weaving straight

Invariably, you will see humps or depressions in the leading edge of the rug (fig. 52). This is the result of warps drifting closer together and the rows of knots not compacting well in that area. This, in turn, is caused by either (1) too little weft resulting in warps drifting together or (2) not beating the rows of knots down enough in that area, or both. The correction lies in being sure that there is ample weft but not too much. Assuming there is enough weft, you can correct the humps by beating the knots down harder in the area of the hump (not too hard or you will break the weft). Similarly, if there are low areas in the center or on either edge of the rug, beat the knots down with less force or not at all until that part of the rug catches up. A heavy, lead-weighted beater helps to ensure a uniform compaction of the rows of knots.

Problems with woolen warp

The natural fuzziness of the warp material tends to create two problems: (1) the woolen weft sticks to the warp, and (2) if the warps are too close together, the warps stick to one another when the sheds are changed and prevent formation of a perfect shed. One of the front warps will be stuck

previous row. In this way, mistakes in the previous row will be discovered and can be corrected without too much trouble. If an error is discovered in the previous row of knots, just pull the two wefts up over the mistake, remove the knots, and re-tie them with the proper color of yarn. You can do this easily using a 2½-inch strand of the pile material and tying the knot with a crochet hook. Then beat the weft down and continue with the next row (fig. 51).

Repairing Broken Warps

When a warp breaks in the process of making the rug, the first things to do is examine your beater. It may be that it has a rough edge on the teeth and needs to be sandpapered. When the warp breaks, it is possible to splice it quite easily. Trace the broken warp string up above the heddles, take an adequate length of warp, and tie a secure, double knot to the end of the broken warp. If the broken warp is a back one, direct it through the heddle corresponding to the broken warp and bring it down to the leading edge of the rug. Make sure that the spliced warp is in the proper space of the broken warp. If it is a front warp, make sure that it goes in front of dowel 3, and if it is a back warp that it goes behind dowel 3. Take a crochet hook and go to a point two inches immediately below the space where the broken warp belongs. Go through the rug to the back side with a crochet hook and engage the spliced warp with the crochet hook and pull it through the rug to the front surface.

Now the warp is in the proper space, and it is possible to tie it under tension so that you can resume weaving. If the leather strap has already been nailed in place, use a crochet hook to pull the new warp behind the leather strap and then pull it up in front of the leather strap and tie it to itself under the proper tension. If the leather strap is not yet in place, because the rug has just been started, get the new warp in the proper space behind the rug and tie it around dowel 1 or the lower beam (fig. 54).

If warp threads become frayed, loose, or broken when you are within two inches of completing your rug, the method described above of splicing the warps is not applicable. With such a small amount of the rug remaining, it is likely that the spliced warp would not be securely anchored in the rug by the series of knots and that warp thread in the fringe might pull out of the rug, making the knots less secure. So if you see a warp thread either very frayed or loose toward the end of the rug, it is best to tie the knots around the pair of warp threads, including the frayed one, and a third warp thread from an adjacent pair. The next knot over can be tied on the pair, one string of which was used for the previous knot, but this does not spoil the accuracy of the design. If the warp thread breaks completely toward the end of the rug, just use the remaining one of the pair and tie it to one thread of an adjacent pair until the rug is finished.

After three inches or so of knots are tied, the spliced warp is well enough secured in the body of the rug by the rows of knots that it may be cut loose from where it was anchored. If you look carefully at many new Oriental rugs, you will see warp threads coming out of the back surface of the rug in various places. These are warps that were broken and spliced. After you have finished the rug, the portion of the warp thread used for splicing will be visible on the back of the rug. One end of the visible warp leads through the rug, and the loose end of it will be in the pile where the warp was cut loose from the loom. That end may be pulled through to the back side of the rug, and then the warp can be cut off

53. *Sticking together of woolen warp pairs can be prevented by use of forearm to push front warps backward.*

to the back warp and the weft will be incorrectly inserted. Problem 1 is solved by laying in the looser weft in short segments to decrease friction between weft and warp as the available weft goes between the warps properly. It is helpful to accentuate the depth of the shed by depressing the front warp threads backward above the heddles (fig. 53). It is also helpful before packing in the loose weft to strum the warps with the fingernails to be sure that the shed is open. In my experience, there is no problem with the warps sticking to one another when the shed is changed, as long as the warps are no closer than eight pairs per inch.

It is interesting that authors of books on rugs often comment that many tribal rugs have warps spaced seven to eight pairs per inch and that the weavers achieve greater density of the pile by having twelve to eighteen rows of knots vertically. This gives the design a flattened, elongated form. I am certain that the reason for this technique is that the tribal rugs were made with woolen warps. The weavers found that about eight pairs per inch was workable and that closer spacing made weft insertion difficult for the reasons mentioned above. This is an original observation, to the best of my knowledge. Another myth about Oriental rugs is that rugs made with woolen warp and weft do not lie flat. Nest Rubio, my friend in Cambridge, England, makes beautiful rugs that lie perfectly flat, and she never uses anything but woolen warp and weft. When you use cotton warp and weft, neither of the two problems mentioned above occurs, since the cotton is quite slick and not sticky.

__54.__ The spliced warp is placed in the proper space, brought through the body of the rug and secured to dowel 1.

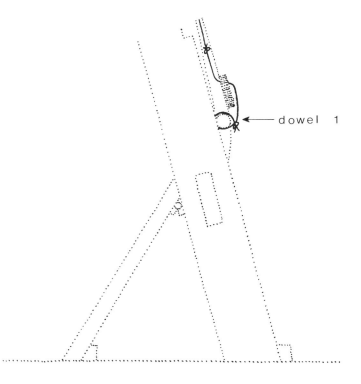

flush with the back of the rug.

Preventing bowing in the weaving

When starting the rug, nail No. 16 common 3½-inch nails below either end of dowel 1 and below the center of dowel 1. Drive these in about an inch and a half. If this is not done, the beating down of the rows of knots will warp the center of dowel 1 downward and the rug will bow downward in the middle. This defect is often seen in the first portion of many larger Oriental rugs. The bowing down in the center occurs before enough rug has been woven to nail the carpet to the loom with the leather strap. The deformity is corrected as the rug weaving progresses.

After about six inches of the rug are woven, the tension on the warps should be loosened by removing the wedges or loosening the bolts, depending on which loom you are using. Then the completed section of the rug, which is about six inches high, is placed over the front of the lower beam and tension is reestablished.

At this point the rug is nailed to the lower beam using a ⅛-inch thick piece of leather three inches high and as wide as the rug. First place the piece of leather on a rough wooden surface and drive 1-inch brass nails with smooth points through the leather as shown in figure 55A. Then place the leather over the completed portion of the rug and drive the small brass nails through the rug at right angles into the lower beam but leave enough nail heads showing for easy removal (fig. 55B). It is a good idea to start in the center and then gradually progress to either side in a zigzag fashion, first to the right and then to the left, a few nails at a time.

The points of the nails must be smooth and the nails driven in at right angles to minimize the chance of severing a warp or weft. They should be brass so that the humidity will not cause rust staining of the rug. If the leather is not nailed in place, the rug will continue to bow downward in the center.

Each time the warps are loosened and the rug is slid to the back of the loom, the leather must be renailed. If a small length of nail head projects above the leather surface, the nail can be removed easily with vise-grip pliers.

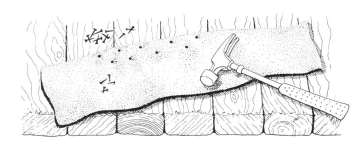

__55A.__ Rest the leather strap on a wooden plank and hammer brass nails through it.

__55B.__ The leather strap is nailed in place to prevent bowing of this Kashan rug (Design 9).

CHAPTER 3

Rug Construction

Making a Sample

Your first attempt at a knotted pile Oriental style rug should be a sample. By making a sample you will master most of the details of technique without wasting a large amount of valuable yarn. By the time you have finished your first sample, you should be able to make one of the smaller rugs shown at the back of the book. Select one that can be completed in sixty to a hundred hours for your initial attempt. It is important that your first rug be a success; otherwise you may get discouraged and abandon a hobby that can give you great satisfaction.

For the sample, select one design from any of the designs in the book. The major design in the Talish rug is a good one to start with. Follow the instructions in Chapter 2 on warping the loom. I would suggest that for your first sample you use fishnet twine 12/6.

Preparing the loom for weaving

Step 1: Start the warping process about 5 inches to the left of the center of dowel 1. The first warp on the left should be a back one. The last warp on the right must be a front one. Use the spacer to prevent bowing of the dowel and follow the instructions carefully in Chapter 2. If you elect not to use a spacer, tie a piece of soft, heavy twine around dowel 1 and the lower beam. You should stretch 85 pairs of front and back warps across the central 8½ inches of dowel 1 with ten warp pairs per inch. This leaves you 81 warp pairs for the knots and two pairs of warps on either side for selvage.

Step 2: When all the back warps are tied forward with heddles and the sheds have been tested, saw through dowel 1 about one inch inside the vertical beam on the right and the left sides (fig. 56). *Measure and record the distance between the movable horizontal beam and the center beam.*

Step 3: Insert the hydraulic jack and remove the wedge on the left side of the loom (or, for loom 2, loosen the bolts on the upper beam to allow downward displacement of the up-

per beam). At this point you should also remove the wedge on the right side of the loom and remove both of the blocks below the horizontal beam on the right and left sides. This is the block in the slot that was placed there for stability during warping (fig. 24). If the loom with a movable upper beam is being used (loom 2), remove the blocks above the upper beam on both sides.

Step 4: With the movable upper or lower horizontal beam loosened, the warps are loose enough to allow downward movement of dowel 1 to the midportion of the front surface of the lower beam (fig. 57). Dowel 1 should be parallel to the lower beam.

Step 5: Reestablish a tension on the warps that exceeds the previous warping tension. If the working distance between the movable horizontal beam and the middle beam was 15 inches, you will probably need to increase that distance to 15¼ or 15½ inches to get the proper tension for weaving. To do this, place the wooden block and wedge up

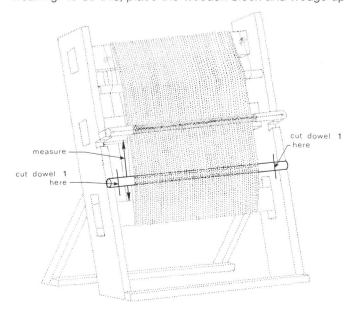

measure

cut dowel 1 here

cut dowel 1 here

56. *Cut through dowel 1 as indicated.*

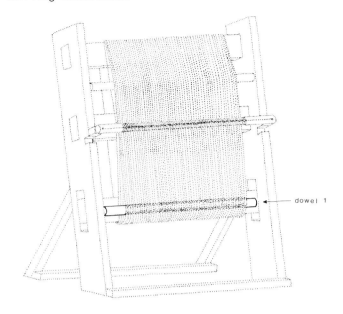

57. *Loosen the movable beam and move dowel 1 to midportion of the beam.*

above the lower horizontal beam in the slot on the right side. It will then probably not be possible to get either the block or the wedge into the slot on the left side without using the hydraulic jack. Place the jack on the 4 x 4 x 6-inch block which is placed on top of the lower beam, and with the jack displace the lower beam downward to a point where you can insert both the wooden block and the wedge. The wedge should be inserted for only about one inch. Then the jack may be removed and the wedges on either side driven in until the distance between the middle and lower beams is approximately ¼ to ½ inch greater than it was when you completed the warping procedure. It is important that both the dowel and the lower beam be an equal distance from the middle beam on the right and left sides. If the movable upper beam loom is used, tighten the nuts on the threaded rods alternately on either side until the tension on the warps is increased by ¼ to ½ inch. In either case the warps should be very taut.

Step 6: Now nail a heavy 3½-inch nail (No. 16 common) 1½ inches into the lower beam just below either end of dowel 1 and another nail just below the center of dowel 1. Be careful to go between the warps with the center nail. These three nails prevent subsequent downward bowing of the dowel (fig. 58).

Step 7: With dowel 3 in the upper position (shed #2), insert into the shed two leash sticks—pieces of balsa wood 12 inches long, 2 inches wide, and ¼ inch thick (fig. 59). Two are inserted instead of one to facilitate later removal. The leash sticks are easier to insert if the ends are rounded off with

sandpaper. The four vertical inches of warp isolated by the leash sticks preserve enough length of warp to tie as fringe when the sample is completed.

Step 8: Nail a 2-inch nail into the front of the vertical beams on either side, just above the top of the leash stick and at equal distances, right and left, below the bottom of the middle beam (fig. 60).

Step 9: Cut a length of string used for warp and make it about two feet longer than twice the width of the loom. Double this and loop it around the nail on the left side, with the midportion of the string looped around the nail. Tie the other two ends of the string around the end of the shuttle so that there is no slack in either string (fig. 61). Now twist the two strings tightly as shown in figure 62.

Step 10: Depress dowel 3 to shed #1, the lower position. Guide the twisted string through this shed and hold it under tension as you beat it down to a straight line between the two nails that are on the front of the vertical beams (see step 8).

Step 11: Tie the string around the nail on the right side of the loom under as much tension as possible. This twisted string acts as a starting point for the rug (fig. 63).

Congratulations! You are now ready to make your first Oriental rug. First comes a double check. Is dowel 1 parallel to the middle beam? Are the leash sticks and twisted string parallel to the middle beam, and is the twisted string straight and under tension? Is the shed open with no stragglers (back warps not tied far enough forward)? If the answer to all these questions is yes, you are ready to weave.

Rug Construction

Weaving the heading. Any good Oriental rug has a webbing or heading before the first row of knots. It takes little time to make, and prolongs the life of the rug immensely. A ½- to 1-inch heading will remain intact for twenty to thirty

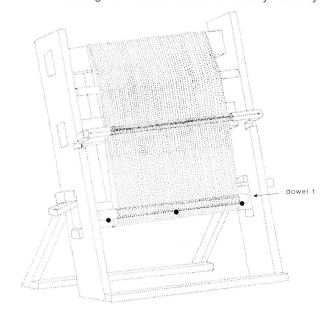

58. *After tension is reestablished, nail No. 16 common nails below center and at either end of dowel 1 as shown.*

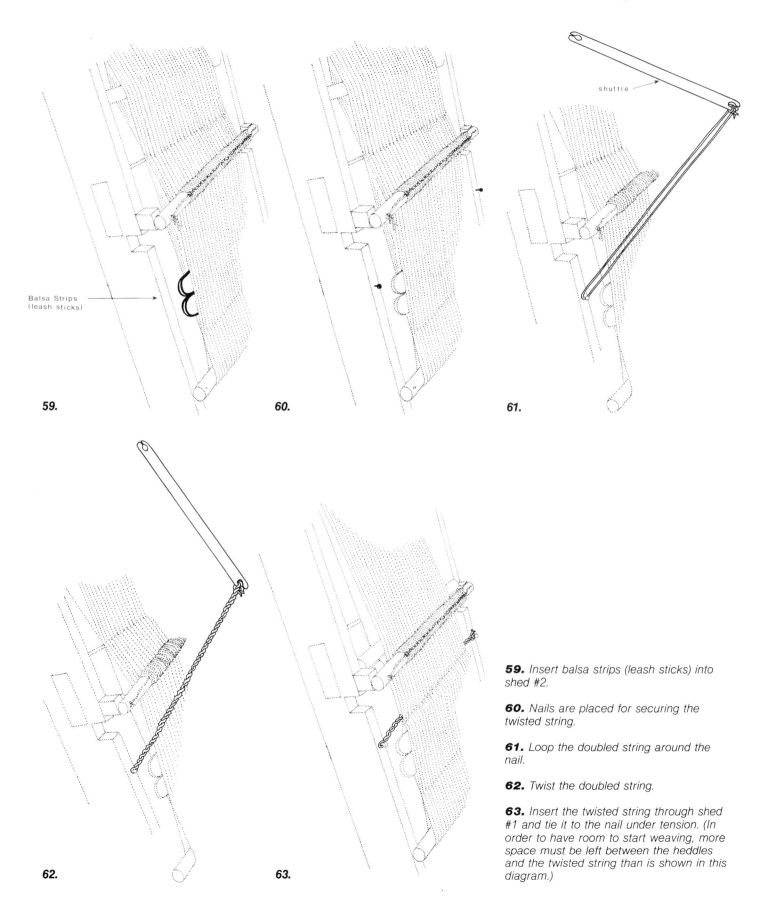

59. *Insert balsa strips (leash sticks) into shed #2.*

60. *Nails are placed for securing the twisted string.*

61. *Loop the doubled string around the nail.*

62. *Twist the doubled string.*

63. *Insert the twisted string through shed #1 and tie it to the nail under tension. (In order to have room to start weaving, more space must be left between the heddles and the twisted string than is shown in this diagram.)*

years or longer and prevent the first row of knots from coming undone. Many rugs that have been made in Iran since 1970 have no heading, merely the twisted, heavy, doubled string over which the fringe is tied, then the first row of knots. But the better Iranian rugs are made by experienced weavers who know the value of this webbing and begin and end their rugs with a heading.

To start the heading, wind as much 12/6 twine as you can on the shuttle and still be able to pass the shuttle through the shed. Tie the end of the string for the beginning of the heading to the nail on the left side of the front of the loom (the same nail used for the twisted string). Reverse the shed to shed #2 (dowel in the upper position) and put the shuttle through the shed. Unwind enough weft to allow the shuttle to be rested above the heddles, and beat down the weft as follows: hold the weft loosely to the right of the warps at an angle of about 30 degrees. Use the butt end of a crochet hook to create bubbles about an inch high and an inch wide across the width of the rug. Use the crochet hook to break these into smaller bubbles, and beat the weft down with the weighted comb. Go across the warps several times with the beater to be sure all weft is down. Reverse the shed to #1 and pass the shuttle from right to left. This is done with the dowel in the lower position. Be sure to pass the weft around the outer pairs of warps that later will be used for selvage. Pack down bubbles of the same size as in the left-to-right passage of weft and again beat down the weft with the weighted comb. (Be sure to put weft in loosely enough to avoid pulling together of warps, a mistake that makes the beginning of the rug narrower than the remainder.) Continue alternating sheds and weaving the heading until the heading is approximately ¾ inch high and the last weft has exited on the right side of the rug. At that point dowel 3 is in the upper position, shed #2.

Starting the selvage. Make two small skeins of the 7/2 wool which has been doubled to become four-ply and is the same color as your background color. Tie a Ghiordes knot around the third pair of warps from the right and left sides of the rug, and then wind these skeins in a figure 8 four times around the outer two pairs of warps (fig. 48). If your selvage binding is the same color as the border background color, the beginning, ending, or splicing knots on the third pair of warps will not be as visible as they would if the binding were a color different from the background color.

Preparing pile yarn. The yarn for the pile should be two-ply 7/2 wool, doubled to four-ply in most cases. The easiest way to get that four-ply yarn is to use a Swedish umbrella swift. First, place a skein of yarn on the swift and leave the yarn end on the floor next to it; then back down the hallway or some other straight passageway the length of your house, unwinding the yarn as you go. When you reach the end of the line, so to speak, pick up the yarn and double it so that it is now four-ply, then wind it around your first and third fingers to make a small skein as you slowly walk back

toward the swift. When you reach the swift, you should break off the yarn and pick the other end of the yarn up off the floor, thus completing your skein of doubled yarn. Continue the process to make as many four-ply skeins as you need.

Tying the knots. With dowel 3 in the #2 shed position, go from left to right and tie a Ghiordes knot around each pair of front and back warps, using the background color. Ghiordes knots are tied as shown in figure 64. Always encircle the front warp first. (The front warp of each pair is to the right of the back warp.) If you tie a Ghiordes knot with one depressed warp, the front warp will be depressed. If you tie a Senna knot (fig. 65), encircling the front warp ensures that the encircled warp will be toward the surface of the rug. If you are left-handed, you will find it easier to encircle the left of each pair of warps as you tie the knot. This will be a back warp. This technique makes no change in the configuration of the Ghiordes knot: the front warp is still depressed and both are encircled. With the left-handed Senna knot, the encircled warp is a back one and is toward the back of the rug (fig. 46).

In Iran and Turkey, weavers work with pile yarn suspended across the upper part of the loom. I find it easier to work from small skeins that lie over the floor with the ends draped across my thighs. You can work with as many as ten colors, with five across each leg.

Beating down the knots. Depress dowel 3 to shed #1 position. Beat down the first row of knots with the weighted comb. Because the teeth of the comb are not as fine as the spacing of the warp threads, it is necessary to go back and forth over the width of the rug several times until all the knots appear to be uniformly beaten down.

Passing the taut weft. Keep dowel 3 in shed #1 position. Run the shuttle (the one used for the heading) through shed #1 and beat down the 12/6 weft under slight tension. As you beat down the weft, look for places where the weft has gone in front of the front warp or behind the back warp. If this

64. Ghiordes knot

1. Stretch the pair of warps over the left index and third fingers.
2. Guide the end of the yarn under the right-side warp with the left index finger.
3. Grasp the end of the yarn between the right index finger and the thumb and pass it in front of the left warp by grasping the yarn with the left index finger and thumb.
4. Pass behind the left warp and up between the left and right warps to deliver the yarn to the right index finger and thumb.
5. Pull the knot down taut.
6. Cut yarn with the paring knife, which you have held in your palm during the knotting procedure. For a ⅜-inch pile rug, cut pile with the knife so that it is over ½ inch high. Trim later.

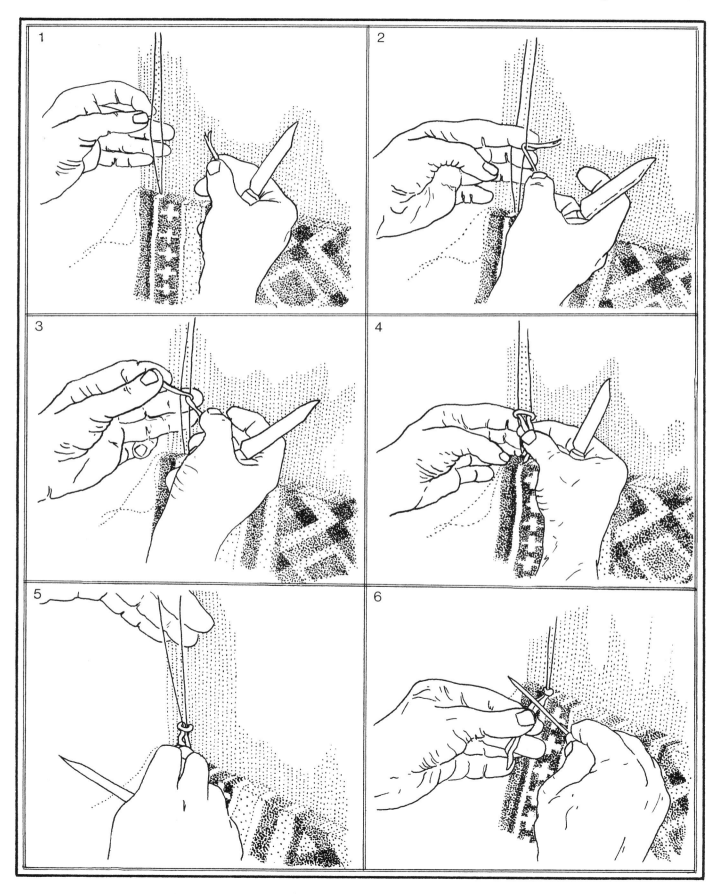

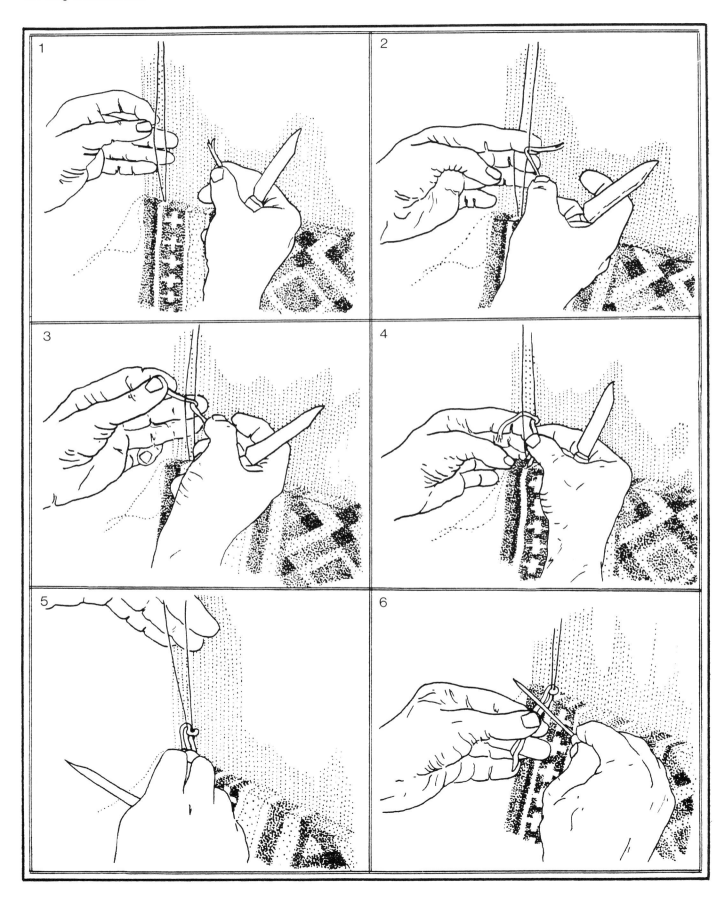

65. Senna knot

1. Stretch the pair of warps over the left index and third fingers.
2. Guide the end of the yarn under the right-side warp with the left index finger.
3. Pass the yarn end under the left warp and grasp with the left index finger and thumb.
4. Transfer yarn end to right index finger and thumb.
5. Grasp the two ends of the pile yarn and pull the knot down tightly.
6. Cut pile yarn with the knife as for the Ghiordes knot.

---

has happened, it will be fairly obvious: there will not be a regular, repetitive interval of weft between the warp threads. To correct the problem, remove the weft back to the point where the error was made and reinsert it. The error probably occurred because two warps stuck together or because a heddle is either too tight or too loose. If this is the case, retie the heddle to the poorly placed warp thread. No slack should be present in the taut weft, but it should not be tight enough to pull the sides of the rug in. The weft must enter and exit between the first and second pairs of warps.

Passing the loose weft. Tie the end of a skein of 12/6 fishnet twine onto your second shuttle. Now wind the shuttle full of this 12/6 twine. The winding should be continued until a large amount of weft is on the shuttle, but so that the shuttle can still easily go through the shed. Use a granny knot to tie the free end of the 12/6 twine to the next-to-last pair of warps on the right side of the rug.

Change to shed #2 (front warps in back and back warps in front) and pass the weft through the shed. The open shed is most easily seen from just above the heddles. This is the deepest portion of the shed. It helps to lay the shuttle for the taut weft on your forearm as you use your forearm to push the front warps backward (fig. 53). Then the open shed #2 is easily seen as the shuttle goes through it. With a crochet hook, make bubbles about one inch high and one inch wide. Make into smaller bubbles with the crochet hook and beat down with the comb. (Also see the alternative method,

"A Good Technique for Weft Insertion," in Chapter 2.)

Once again, look for errors in weft passage. It will take a while to discern whether you are putting in too much weft or too little. Err on the side of too much. If you are holding the weft loosely at a 45-degree angle, as you create bubbles with the crochet hook, more weft will go in than if you hold the weft at a lesser angle. If too much weft is going in, you will see excessive amounts of weft protruding between the rows of knots on the back side of the rug (fig. 66). When this happens, decrease the angle for the loose weft, while creating bubbles.

As the weft exits on the left side of the rug, it must come out between the first and second pairs of warps. When the weft on the shuttle is depleted, knot it and rewind the weft onto the shuttle. The knot in the weft should be on the surface of the rug rather than on the back. The ends of the knot will be buried in the pile, and the ends of the weft splicing can be cut off slightly shorter than the pile, so that they will not show as a light colored knot in the rug. If you look carefully at any Oriental rug, you will find frequent splicings of the weft or even warp, as evidenced by knots buried in the pile of the rug.

Winding the selvage. After the weft has been passed from right to left under tension, and then from right to left loosely, wrap the doubled selvage yarn (four-ply) in a figure 8 fashion around the outer two pairs of warp threads on the right side of the rug, using five or six complete figure 8s. This creates a nice binding and hides the weft threads, which engage the next-to-last pair of warp threads. The wrapping of the selvage is always done on the side opposite where the wefts exit and should be slightly higher than the recently completed row of knots.

---

66. *(A) This diagram shows the proper amount of weft. (B) If too much weft is inserted, loops of weft show on the back side of the rug. (C) Too little weft pulls the warps closer together and tends to prevent good compacting of the rows of knots. Thus a bulge develops in the leading edge of the rug.*

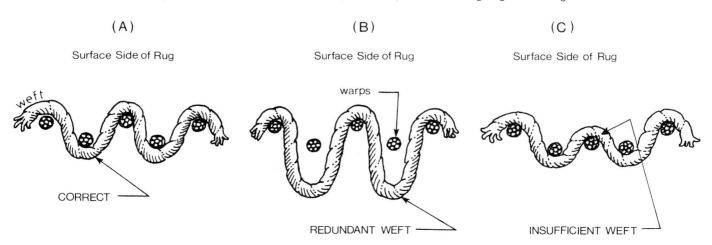

(A)   (B)   (C)

Surface Side of Rug   Surface Side of Rug   Surface Side of Rug

CORRECT   REDUNDANT WEFT   INSUFFICIENT WEFT

67. This crude blade is used to shave the damp surface of fine carpets in the Orient.

Cutting the pile. Before cutting the recently completed row of knots, it is important to brush the pile down with your hands so that it is perpendicular to the weft threads. After the design has started, you will see why this is important. If the pile is allowed to remain slanted to right or left, the design may be slightly distorted after the next row of knots is placed.

Cut the completed row of knots the desired height of the pile. Check for accuracy with a short wooden measuring stick. After an inch or so of the rug is woven, it is easy to control the height of the pile by resting the lower blade of the scissors firmly on the surface of the rug during cutting. It is usually necessary to make two passes with the scissors to get even trimming.

It is a good idea to check the height of the pile and the width of the rug after each row of knots is cut. If the rug is getting slightly narrower, grasp the outer four inches of the rug and pull it outward. Repeat this maneuver on the other edge. If you have enough weft in, this will prevent progressive narrowing of the rug.

Continuing the weaving. With shed #2 open (dowel 3 elevated), tie the second row of knots, excluding the outer two pairs of warp threads on either side for selvage. Change to shed #1, brush the pile down straight with your hand, and beat the row of knots down with the weighted comb.

Pass the taut weft through the shed from left to right, not engaging the outer pair of warps on either side. This is done with shed #1, with the dowel in the downward position. Beat down the taut weft under moderate tension but without pulling in the sides of the rug.

Pass the loose weft from left to right through shed #2, creating bubbles as before. Beat down the weft and inspect the back of the rug to see if there are excessive amounts of weft present between the first two rows of knots. Make the necessary adjustments.

Wind the figure 8s of the selvage five or six times around the outer two pairs of warps on the left side of the rug.

Now, mark the center of the warps (43rd pair of warps from either side) with a pencil. Decide where you want your design to start. The major Talish design is 41 knots wide at its widest point, so you might want 20 rows of plain-colored knotting before starting the design. On the 21st row, tie a dark brown knot on the center warp to mark the beginning of the design.

As the rug progresses, correct problems by referring to Chapter 2. If you are doing everything right, the leading edge of the weaving should be straight, the width of the sample should remain the same, and the length of the sample should remain the same on both sides. If any of these measurements are off, make corrections as outlined in Chapter 2. If you measure the height of each row of pile after trimming and trim again as needed, your rug surface will remain smooth.

Do not be discouraged if the surface of the rug looks granular and the rows of knots stand out. Part of this is from your perspective of looking at the rug in a vertical position. The principal reason for the graininess is that the pile is standing erect and has some fuzz on the surface. After you have walked on the rug for six months or so, the surface will become smoother and the pile matted down until it becomes "one pile." This smooth surface is the desired effect in an Oriental rug. In Iran, the very finest in closely knotted rugs are shaved after the end of the weaving procedure. This is done by wetting down the surface of the pile with water and then shaving in the direction of the slope of the pile with a sharp blade (figs. 67 and 68). I have not found this to be necessary for the rugs described in this book.

68. The rug shaver in use

Moving the rug down on the loom. When you reach a point where the edge of the weaving is about eight inches below the heddles, you will appreciate the need for moving the rug downward on the loom. At that point it will be difficult to grasp the divergent front and back warp threads in preparation for tying the knots. To move the rug downward, the following steps are necessary:

Step 1: Remove the nails below dowel 1 and take off the tension on the warp threads by removing the wedges on either side. If your loom has a movable lower beam, it will probably be necessary to insert the jack to extract the wedge on the left side. The wedge on the right side can then be removed by hand.

Step 2: Remove the leash sticks and cut loose the twisted string that was placed for the beginning of the heading. Also cut the beginning of the heading thread loose from the nail on the left side of the loom.

Step 3: Move dowel 1 to the back of the loom until the leading edge of the rug is just ¼ inch above the top of the lower horizontal beam. Then reestablish tension and check it by measuring the distance between the movable beam and the middle beam. Nail a leather strap (⅛ inch thick and 3 inches high and as wide as the rug) to the front of the loom through the rug with brass nails (see p. 36). One thing that I have not mentioned is that when the rug is moved to the back of the loom, the process tends to distort the heddles and pull them downward. Before reestablishing tension it is important to push the heddles up to a position directly behind dowel 2, instead of leaving them in their depressed position below dowel 2. If the tension in the warp threads is reestablished with the heddles depressed downward, it may break some of them and distort the warp threads. Before reestablishing tension, with the side of your finger press the heddles up to their original position directly behind dowel 2.

Ending the selvage. After reestablishing the tension, continue weaving until the full 85 rows of knots are completed. At this point you must finish off the rug in preparation for removal from the loom. After the last row of knots is placed, wind the figure 8 selvage on both the right and left sides until it is even with the last row of knots. Tie the end of each selvage to the third pair of warp strings on each side with a Ghiordes knot. Then place the last rows of weft, one tightly and one loosely. Now use the two shuttles to weave the heading. Be sure to engage the outer pairs of warps on either side with the heading weft. After a ¾-inch heading is woven, your sample is finished.

Tying the fringe. Using a wide felt marking pen, draw a straight line across the warps 4 inches above your completed heading. Now cut the warps along this line two pairs at a time. Tie the four warps in a single knot that rests up against the heading (fig. 69). You will soon learn to leave the loop and the knot large, so that you can coax it down to the point where it abuts against the heading. Continue cutting

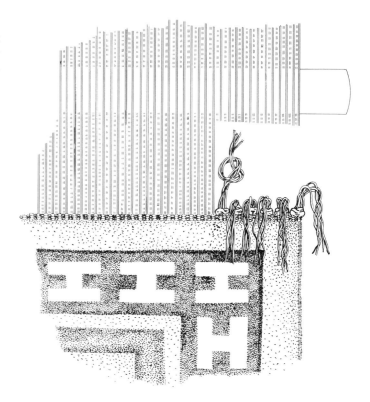

69. *The warps are cut two pairs at a time and are tied in a single knot flush with the last row of knots.*

warps four at a time and tying the knots until the upper portion of the rug hangs loose and the fringe is all tied. If you leave too little length of warps between two rugs on the same loom, it may not be possible to tie a knot in the fringe. This can be avoided by leaving at least 8 inches between two rugs when two are made on the same loom. However, if you do goof, you can solve the problem by tying a series of half-granny knots continuously around each four warp threads from one side of the rug to the other. This is a little less secure than individually knotted fringe, but it is a good way out of the dilemma.

Taking the rug off the loom. Cut the warps off just above dowel 1 at the beginning of the rug. Tie the beginning heading thread (which was previously tied to the nail on the front of the vertical beam) in with the first two pairs of warps on the left side. Tie the heading threads at the opposite end of the loom in with the fringe. Remove the twisted double string that had been stretched across between the nails. Now tie each of the two pairs of warps against the heading in a single knot just as you did on the other end of the rug (fig. 69).

If the fringe is uneven, trim it at this point. Check the sides and surfaces of the rug and trim off any unruly pile threads that are sticking up. Brush the sample with a stiff brush to improve the appearance of the pile and get rid of any loose wool bits in the surface of the rug.

One final finishing touch will improve the appearance

of your rug. If the weft is a different color from the border selvage, as it usually is, a bit of weft is visible between the selvage and the first row of knots. Because the pile slopes to the left, this weft is not visible on the left side of the rug, but it is visible on the right side. You can use a felt marking pen that matches the selvage color to color the visible weft on the right side of the rug where selvage meets pile.

If your sample is smooth and square and lies flat, you are ready to make any size rug you want. The same steps you use in the sample are used in any size rug. All that differs is the number of warps, the complexity of the pattern, and the number of colors. So choose one of the smaller rugs from the designs in this book or perhaps you would like to use a design from Maggie Lane's books *Needlepoint by Design* and *More Needlepoint by Design* (or her other books). Her patterns are lovely and involve only two to five colors and can be completed in sixty to eighty hours.

Making more than one rug on a loom. You usually have room for more than one rug on the loom. After you finish the first rug, put two 4-inch-wide strips of ¼-inch balsa wood in series between the end of the first rug and the beginning of the second. That way when you finish both rugs, you can cut them apart and still have four inches of warp to tie as fringe on each of the rugs. Whenever you are using the balsa wood dividers between rugs or at the beginning of the rug, these pieces of wood must be removed before the rug and warps will negotiate the turn around the underside of the lower beam. Before moving the rug, take the tension off the warp strings and slip the leash sticks out, so that the rug and warps can easily be turned around to the back of the loom for continued weaving.

CHAPTER 4

Colors and Designs

Colors

The skillful use of colors in making your own Oriental rugs comes with experience. But there are some general considerations I have arrived at over the past years that might be helpful as you start using various colors in Oriental rugs.

Color selection. Color in Oriental rugs is really a form of expression. I have looked at hundreds of Oriental rugs, and each one usually says something to me. The rug may be somber in appearance. Certainly many of the old Turkomans and Beluchistans were quite dark, with their deep mahogany browns mixed with burgundy, red, deep turquoise, and navy blue. Many of the Beluchistans have just a small dash of beige in the dark background, and it stands out like a jewel on a dark velvet dress.

Then there are the bright and happy rugs. One thinks immediately of Caucasian rugs. The nice thing about them is that they are not at all subtle. There is a lot of contrast between the generally harmonious reds, yellows, greens, golds, blues, and beiges.

The message of many Chinese rugs is one of simplicity and subtle harmony, like the tones of a symphony orchestra. There may be no more than five or six colors, or even fewer, in the lovely old Chinese rugs, and sometimes all the colors except one are various shades of blue. Their subtlety and uncomplicated grace and their depth of beauty are reminiscent of Chinese culture and the people themselves.

Many old floral Persian rugs speak to us with a message of sophisticated elegance and complexity. If you study the older Kashans or Isfahans you will often see as many as fifteen colors. Usually there are four or more shades of red and blue, several shades of green, and a lovely background of a creamy beige which is made by dyeing the yarn lightly with henna. These colors blend together and speak to us softly through the intricate floral designs.

In many Oriental rugs one color is dominant and can be enhanced if it is used as a focal point in decorating. If you make a rug for your own home, I would suggest that you choose a dominant color to go with the decor somewhere in your house. There is usually a perfect place for every rug and the challenge is to find that place.

Introduction of colors. In Chapter 5, specific colors are selected for the weaver. By following the instructions, you can make your rug look like the rug in the color plate. As you become more experienced and a bit daring, you may want to choose different colors, either for the designs in this book or for some other rug you want to make.

The first step is to determine how many colors you need for the rug. Then decide what color substitutions you want to make. When you have selected all the colors, place skeins of the different yarns together and determine if they are compatible. Also consider if the colors look good in the room where you plan to use the rug.

When you are satisfied with your choice for the background color and the various other colors, reexamine your selections. If you have chosen wisely, you will have colors that are gradually introduced in the outer minor borders and then are used more freely in the center of the rug. By the time you weave the second minor border, you should have introduced most of the colors. Most colors need a friend. If you have blue in the rug, it works nicely to have several shades of blue gradually introduced, from rich warm tones to cool light ones. The same is true of greens and reds if the design is complex enough to accommodate that many colors.

By recomposing colors in a rug you can greatly alter its tone and effect. Study design 1 and try to imagine it in the alternate colors listed. Design 8 is beautiful as pictured. It would be equally striking with a navy blue background for the center field. If this were done, some of the colors of the stars would have to be changed to show up well on the darker background. Design 8 is also very attractive with a plain dark blue field without the stars. If you choose to make several color versions of the rugs in Chapter 5, I wish you a long life. You will need the time.

Availability of suitable colors in the United States. Certainly I am not suggesting that we have the wools and color choices available in the United States to make all types of Oriental rugs, but there are many kinds of Oriental rugs within the capability of the American weaver using available wools.

Caucasian rugs are no problem. Many of our companies have a wide selection of compatible basic colors for the bright geometric rugs of the Caucasus. You can get a fairly good selection from Harrisville yarns and a wider selection from the Scandinavian tuna garn. The nice thing about Caucasian rugs is that even the older ones still are bright and cheery, and the replica will look very authentic.

Beluchistan, Turkoman, and other somber tribal rugs likewise maintain their rich, dark colors over the years. So if you make a copy of one of these rugs and use dark maroons, browns, turquoise, navy blue, and deep reds, your rug will look quite realistic.

Tribal rugs such as those from the Qashgai and Kurdish areas are not quite as bright as the Caucasian rugs, but they do use fairly bold colors. These colors hold up well over the years, and your copy of a Kurdish or other tribal rug will look much like the original. These tribal rugs use some odd combinations such as maroon and red, orange, green, beige, and some shades of blue. Since I am not fond of using orange with maroon and red, I generally select a deep gold or some orangish shade of red in place of the orange.

Yarns are available for authentic replicas of Chinese rugs. It is easy to find five or more shades of blue in 7/2 wool (tuna garn). With these you can make lovely floral or geometric Chinese rugs.

There are some limitations in what sorts of floral Persian rugs one can make with the yarns available. One of the main limiting factors is the availability of a suitable beige. The beige in most floral Persian rugs is a delicate cream color made by dyeing the natural wool with henna. I have been unable to find wool this color from the sources available in the United States. I tried dyeing the natural colored wool with tea, but it turned out a dirty brown. The Scandinavian wools do come in a silver beige, which is seen in the rug I copied from a Turkish tapestry (plate C). This is quite satisfactory as a beige for use in floral rugs, but it is not as pretty as the cream beige.

Authentic looking colors. You will generally have the greatest success making an authentic looking floral Persian rug if you stick with dark colors as in the floral Kashan rug (plate I). Even the older dark-shaded floral Persian rugs maintain their colors through the years, so a replica made from new yarn can look quite authentic as long as you don't use much beige in it. It is too early to tell if the colors in the rugs I make will soften with the passage of time. I hope they will. I try to put my new rugs in the sunshine near a window or a door, hoping that the sun will mellow the colors a little. So far, three years' exposure of the Talish rug has not softened the colors at all. Another thing that makes floral rugs look authentic is to use the outlining technique seen in so many floral Persian rugs. Each flower is usually outlined in one or perhaps two colors. On a red or dark blue background perhaps brown and beige will be used as the outlining colors. On a red background, blue in two shades will be used as an outlining color. This prevents the flower from sticking out like a sore thumb on a sharply contrasting color. An intermediate shade between the flower and the background color softens the effect and is responsible for much of the charm and subtlety of floral Persian rugs.

As you copy Oriental rugs, you may be able to improve on the colors. In one rug (plate F) I changed the original orange to a deep gold and liked the rug much better. Some of the tribal rugs particularly have a poor choice of colors, and anyone with a sense for colors can often improve on the color scheme of the rug while copying it. The colors indicated for the designs in this book are merely suggestions. As you gain experience combining colors you will probably be able to improve on my choices. Certainly there is a wide range of preferences for colors and considerable variety of home decor. The colors I chose suit the decor of my home. Part of the fun is to be creative while copying the work of another artist.

Designs: General information

When you have mastered the basic technique of Oriental rug weaving, you will be ready to make a rug with a design in it. Different designs appeal to different people. Most Americans are not immediately attracted to brightly colored Oriental rugs with busy patterns. When I lived in Iran, I was like most Americans and liked the pastel rugs with simpler patterns. The first room-sized rug my wife and I purchased was a 9 x 12 foot Kashan with an overall beige background and muted pastel design. Without exception our Iranian friends were appalled at our choice. They kept asking *Kam rang nist?* ("Isn't it too pale?"). Finally we learned that white is the color of mourning in Iran, the land of opposites. Our pale rug made our Iranian friends feel sad, but we liked it. Little by little we learned to like the brighter rugs, and perhaps you will too.

Selecting a design. I would encourage you to select a fairly simple design for your first rug. I highly recommend Maggie Lane's books *Needlepoint by Design* and *More Needlepoint by Design*, which supply many needlepoint patterns taken from Chinese rug patterns. I have reversed the process and am reconverting her needlepoint designs into Chinese rugs. The designs are quite easy to follow from her books.

When using the designs in this book, be sure to have them enlarged for easier reading. To keep your place as you weave, put a mark beside each row on the design as you finish it.

Copying existing rugs. If you prefer to use designs

other than the ones in this book, you may rely on a number of sources. For example, the Talish rug in plate H is a copy of a rug I found rolled up in Bill Knadjian's rug store three years ago. This is a very rare rug and is not often found in good condition. This particular Talish in his store had been left for repairs. I spent two hours copying the major designs on graph paper, and then all I had to do was measure the intervals between the various designs and the borders and count the knots across the width of the rug and I was ready to copy it without actually having the rug at hand.

The two Shiraz mats pictured in plates A and D and the Qashgai rug pictured in plate F were copied from rugs I had purchased.

Mixing and matching. I arrived at the design of the Gendje mat (plate B) in quite a different way. I found a picture of a Gendje rug in a rug magazine and was able to work out the central design on graph paper. I had an antique Shirvan rug that had a border similar to the one pictured on the Gendje rug, and it was easy to adapt this border to fit the center pattern. Thus I made the rug from a photograph and a borrowed border pattern.

Photographing the back of a rug. The Chinese rug in plate E was arrived at in a rather devious and complicated fashion. I found a 3 x 3 foot Chinese rug in a rug store in Colorado Springs and fell in love with it. But the dealer also loved it—so much that he wouldn't sell it for less than $1,300. My solution was to hire the hotel photographer to take a photograph of the back of the rug. I then took the negatives to a professional photographer at home and had him enlarge the photograph of one quadrant of the rug. From that photograph, and the color photographs that were also taken, my design artist was able to copy the design on graph paper.

More copying experiences. The Kashan rug pictured in plate I was one of a pair I found in the Marco Polo Shop at the Broadmoor Hotel in Colorado Springs. The pair cost $1,500, or $800 apiece. I could afford to buy only one at that time. A few months later I tried to buy the mate and found that the dealer had sequestered it in Denver and refused to sell it. He said he wanted to put it in a museum, and if he ever did sell it, the price would be much higher than for the first one. Instead of trying to persuade him to part with his rug, I spent the next ten months copying the rug I owned, using the back as a pattern. I sent him a photograph of my copy along with a note telling him that if he needed another pair, I would be glad to make them for him. It is a great game having an encounter with an Oriental rug dealer. Many of them take the attitude that they cannot bear to part with certain rugs, and if you want a particular rug badly enough, you must keep offering more and more money.

The Turkoman design, plate G, was one of my earlier efforts. In a how-to-do-it book I suppose it is appropriate at some point to tell "how not to do it." This design is a copy of a fine Turkoman saddle bag. I made this rug before my ses-

70. A close-up of the back of a Yomud Turkoman rug shows errors in warp sharing in the first part of the rug. The technique was mastered later in the rug.

sions with Mrs. Pahlevan and was still making single-wefted rugs that pulled in quite a bit at the top. I might say in my defense that the weaver of the original had some problem with this: the saddle bag is several inches narrower at the top than at the bottom. Also if you look at the back of the original, there are several mistakes in warp sharing, a process by which each knot engages the front thread from one pair of warps from the back pair of the adjacent warps (fig. 70). This results in the diagonal lines going up at a less acute angle than if the pairs were knotted a pair at a time. In any case, I did capture the somber, serious beauty of the Turkoman colors.

The design shown in plate C has two sources. The center portion of the rug is from a Turkish tapestry given to us by Ezra Young, who was with the YMCA in Turkey and Lebanon for thirty-five years. I thought this needlepoint piece was lovely and should be made into a rug. The border is taken from an antique Kashan rug, and I think the two complement one another. With tongue in cheek I call this an Albuturkey design, indicating my home city as well as the tapestry's country of origin.

The Qashgai duck rug (plate F) is another copying story. I have a psychiatrist friend, Dr. Thomas Murray, who is now practicing in Denver. He and I worked together in Iran for three and one-half years. One interesting thing about Dr. Murray is that he is a psychiatrist who is afraid of birds. He can't help it; it is just like a fear of heights. I often think it paradoxical that he is absolutely fearless with dangerously agitated psychiatric patients, but get him around birds and he goes bananas. So for a spoof, I copied a Qashgai duck rug for him last year. By walking on this "therapy rug," I predict his ornithophobia will soon be "defeeted."

Information for each design. The designs in Chapter 5 are arranged in order of complexity, and for each design I have tabulated the following information: (1) pile material, (2) heading, (3) warp, (4) weft, (5) selvage, (6) height of pile, (7) overall size, (8) type of knots, and (9) colors.

To estimate the number of skeins needed for the rug, divide the number of knots by 2,500 (for all rugs except design 9, for which you divide by 5,000). Then estimate the percentage of each color. After you have constructed the Talish sample as described in Chapter 3, it would be a good idea to make some of the smaller rugs before attempting the more difficult designs. I recommend that you make at least two of the designs from Maggie Lane's books, *Needlepoint by Design* and *More Needlepoint by Design*. These charming Chinese mats can be completed more quickly than some of the other designs.

Troubleshooting. I suggest that you review Chapters 2 and 3 before starting any of these rugs and be alert to distortions and errors as they develop. As you begin a rug, frequently measure the number of knots per vertical inch. Adjust tension on warps until the desired number is obtained. This is a critical factor in square rugs, where too much tension on the warps will result in excessive compaction of the rows and a rug that is wider than it is long. Once the desired tension is obtained, record the distance between the fixed and movable beams and reestablish it each time you move the rug to the back of the loom. This will ensure that your designs are of uniform height throughout the rug.

Toward the end of a large rug, you may notice that a greater amount of tension is required for consistent height of the designs. This is the result of stretching of the warp threads over a long period of time. It is necessary to monitor the number of rows for each vertical inch from the beginning to the end of the rug.

By the time you have finished two of the smaller rugs you will be ready for the larger and more complicated ones. The designs indicate the number of knots vertically and horizontally. Always add two extra pairs of warps on each side of the rug for winding selvage. A rug 165 knots wide requires 169 pairs of warps.

I sincerely hope that you enjoy this hobby as much as I have. If you persist in completing the designs of the rugs in this book, I feel certain that you will have a challenging hobby for years to come and that your household will soon be enhanced by beautiful Oriental rugs similar to those found in expensive rug shops. As your skill increases you may want to create your own designs or do rugs with composite designs from several rugs. These same designs can be used for needlepoint.

CHAPTER 5

Design Patterns

Design 1. *Shiraz mat* (plate A)

Design 1 shows the colors and patterns for half of the rug. There is one exception. The half flowers in the center are not to be reproduced as a mirror image in the remaining half. The petals in these flowers alternate between two colors, and this alternation must be continued as you weave the second half of the rug, thus avoiding an error that would occur if you wove a mirror image. The colors in the photograph are not characteristic of rugs from Shiraz. I made this rug to match the bedroom color scheme of the daughter of a medical school classmate of mine. The rug will look more authentic if you use the alternate choice of colors.

Total number of skeins of 7/2 wool needed: 13½

Pile material: 7/2 wool doubled

Heading: 12/9 fishnet twine loose

Warp: 12/9 fishnet twine, seven pairs per horizontal inch (169 pairs, including 4 for selvage)

Weft: 12/9 fishnet twine inserted loosely and 12/9 fishnet twine under tension

Selvage: 7/2 wool doubled, same as background material

Height of pile: ⅜ inch

Overall size: 24 x 22 inches

Type of knots: Ghiordes, nine per vertical inch (200 vertical rows of knots)

Colors (listed in order of predominant use):

☐ 7/2 medium blue #3022
☒ 7/2 medium light blue #3727
⊡ 7/2 pale blue #3085
▣ 7/2 gold #3036
⊞ 7/2 tan #3302
⊡ 7/2 natural beige #3001
☑ 7/2 light green #3008
⊟ 7/2 yellow #3003
⊟ 7/2 dark green #3030
◬ 7/2 dark blue #3013

Alternate

☐ 7/2 dark blue #3013
☒ 7/2 red #3024
⊡ 7/2 medium blue #3022
▣ 7/2 gold #3036
⊞ 7/2 maroon #3027
⊡ 7/2 natural beige #3001
☑ 7/2 pink #3017
⊟ 7/2 yellow #3003
⊟ 7/2 medium green #3010
◬ 7/2 dark brown #3018

Design 2. ***Gendje mat*** (plate B)

Total number of skeins of 7/2 wool needed: 26

Pile material: 7/2 wool doubled

Heading: 12/6 fishnet twine loose

Warp: 12/6 fishnet twine, ten pairs per horizontal inch (213 pairs, including 4 for selvage)

Weft: 12/6 fishnet twine inserted loosely and 12/6 fishnet twine under tension

Selvage: 7/2 wool doubled

Height of pile: $\frac{3}{8}$ inch

Overall size: 21 x 32 inches

Type of knots: Ghiordes, nine to ten per vertical inch (307 vertical rows of knots)

Colors (listed in order of predominant use):

(Refer to the color plate for colors in the design and in the diagonal rows of stars. Reference to the color plate will make it clear what you are to use for outlining colors, background colors, and interior designs.)

- [x] 7/2 dark brown #3018
- [v] 7/2 gold #3036
- [+] 7/2 red #3024
- [○] 7/2 natural beige #3001
- [□] 7/2 medium light blue #3727
- [\] 7/2 pale blue #3085
- [•] 7/2 light green #3008
- [△] 7/2 medium blue #3022
- [■] 7/2 dark blue #3013
- [|] 7/2 tan #3302

Design 3. ***Albuturkey rug*** (plate C)

Total number of skeins of 7/2 wool needed: 23½

Pile material: 7/2 wool doubled

Heading: Navajo warp loose

Warp: Navajo warp, seven pairs per horizontal inch (179 pairs, including 4 for selvage)

Weft: Navajo warp loose and Navajo warp under tension

Selvage: 7/2 wool doubled, same color as background material

Height of pile: $\frac{3}{8}$ inch

Overall size: 25 x 36 inches

Type of knots: Ghiordes, nine to ten per vertical inch (328 rows of vertical knots)

Note: The floral design is different in the four corners.

Colors (listed in order of predominant use):

- [ ] 7/2 silver beige #3304
- [x] 7/2 medium blue #3022
- [○] 7/2 red #3024
- [v] 7/2 tan #3302
- [•] 7/2 medium light blue #3727
- [||] 7/2 dark brown #3018
- [△] 7/2 light green #3008

Design 4. *Shiraz mat* (plate D)

Designs 1 and 4 are from Shiraz and are fairly characteristic of the rugs from that area. Books on Oriental rugs can give you many interesting facts on Shiraz rugs, so I will mention only that the diamond-shaped figure in the center of the smaller rug (design 1) is seen in many Shiraz rugs. In the larger rug (design 4) please note the figure in the center, which is very similar to the Talish design. In rugs from the south of Iran, particularly from the tribal areas around Shiraz and Isfahan, it is striking how many designs are similar to those in Caucasian and Turkish rugs. It is my understanding that many of the tribes that settled in the south of Iran migrated through Turkey and the Caucasus region centuries ago and apparently brought many of their designs with them. The oak leaf and wineglass patterns in the Gendje rug (plate B) are not unlike the stylized design in the Shiraz rug in plate D.

Total number of skeins of 7/2 wool needed: 16

Pile material: 7/2 wool doubled

Heading: 12/9 fishnet twine loose

Warp: 12/9 fishnet twine, eight pairs per horizontal inch (173 pairs, including 4 for selvage)

Weft: 12/9 fishnet twine loose and 12/9 fishnet twine under tension

Selvage: 7/2 wool doubled

Height of pile: ⅜ inch

Overall size: 21 x 29 inches

Type of knots: Ghiordes, eight per vertical inch (236 vertical rows of knots)

Colors (listed in order of predominant use):

☐ 7/2 dark blue #3013
☒ 7/2 orange-red #3015
⊞ 7/2 medium blue #3022
◉ 7/2 honey beige #3303
☑ 7/2 dark brown #3018
△ 7/2 light green #3008
▣ 7/2 red #3024
⊡ 7/2 natural beige #3001

The small dark blue square between the large central designs is also attractive done in dark brown (see color plate). When you are half finished with the rug, the central design can be repeated by reference to the color plate. The border designs should be continued with the motif in the same direction as noted in the color plate.

Design 5. *Chinese rug* (plate E)

Design 5 shows the beauty and simplicity of Chinese rugs. The design is simple, and there is much open space, but the subtle combinations of colors give the rug grace and beauty so characteristic of many Chinese rugs.

Total number of skeins of 7/2 wool needed: 18

Pile material: 7/2 wool doubled

Heading: 12/9 fishnet twine loose

Warp: 12/9 fishnet twine, eight pairs per horizontal inch (221 pairs, including 4 for selvage)

Weft: 12/9 fishnet twine loose and 12/9 fishnet twine under tension

Selvage: 7/2 wool doubled

Height of pile: ⅜ inch

Overall size: 27 x 25 inches

Type of knots: Ghiordes, eight per vertical inch (204 rows of vertical knots)

Colors (listed in order of predominant use):

- ☐ 7/2 gold #3036
- ☒ 7/2 dark blue #3013
- ⊙ 7/2 natural beige #3001
- ⊻ 7/2 medium blue #3022
- ⊡ 7/2 honey beige #3303
- ⊙ 7/2 tan #3302

Design 6. *Qashgai duck rug* (plate F)

Design 6 is a Qashgai rug with a bird design. I copied this charming little rug from a worn-out mat I bought in Santa Fe several years ago. I changed the colors a little from the original because I didn't like the bright orange that was one of the major colors. The overall effect is still consistent with that of a tribal rug from the Qashgai area around Shiraz and Isfahan.

Total number of skeins of 7/2 wool needed: 17

Pile material: 7/2 wool doubled

Heading: Navajo warp loose

Warp: Navajo warp, seven pairs per horizontal inch (167 pairs, including 4 for selvage)

Weft: Navajo warp loose and Navajo warp under tension

Selvage: 7/2 wool doubled, same color as background material

Height of pile: ⅜ inch

Overall size: 24 x 28 inches

Type of knots: Ghiordes, nine to ten per vertical inch (252 rows of vertical knots)

Colors (listed in order of predominant use):

- ☐ 7/2 dark blue #3013
- ☒ 7/2 dark red #3032
- ⊻ 7/2 red #3024
- ⊙ 7/2 maroon #3027
- ⊞ 7/2 dark gold #3049
- ⊡ 7/2 honey beige #3303
- △ 7/2 medium green #3010
- ▣ 7/2 dark brown #3018
- ⊡ 7/2 gold #3036
- ⧄ 7/2 medium blue #3022
- ⧅ 7/2 dark green #3030

Design 7. *Yomud Turkoman bag face* (plate G)

The Turkoman design shown here is adaptable to several different rugs. One can make the rug as shown. This rug is 54 inches wide and requires a loom with an internal width between the vertical beams of about 60 inches. The loom must be the kind with a movable upper beam. If you do not care to make the entire rug, you can make an oblong mat with just three gulls in the center and perhaps leave off the asymmetrical skirt at the bottom, just continuing the border design around on the sides instead. For a small Turkoman you can use Navajo warp seven per horizontal inch, 7/2 wool as loose weft and Navajo warp as a taut weft, and 7/2 wool doubled as pile (see table 1 in Chapter 1).

Because I did not particularly like the flying bird in the major border, I changed that feature so that there are individually distinct figures in the border.

The major border requires detailed explanation. It consists of motifs that are twenty-five knots wide and twenty-five knots high. The background colors of these motifs are red, dark blue, maroon, and dark green (if you select dark brown for the overall background color, use dark brown instead of maroon). Starting at the lower left corner of the rug with a red motif, these figures alternate clockwise around the rug as follows: red, dark blue, maroon, and dark green. Going across the rug there are thirteen motifs at twenty-five knots each, twelve spaces of five knots each, and two end spaces of one knot each—a total of 387 knots.

Going up the side there are fourteen motifs at twenty-three knots each, seven spaces at seven knots each, six spaces at five knots each, and two end spaces with two knots each—a total of 405 knots. The colors of the outlines of these motifs, the colors of the cross in the center, and the color of the center of the cross are listed below in table 3.

The triangles between the motifs are all outlined in maroon (or in dark brown if you choose that for the overall background color). Starting between motifs 1 and 2, the interior colors of the triangles are: red, dark green, red, dark blue, red, dark green, red, dark blue, etc. Once again the rotation starts at the left corner of the rug and proceeds clockwise.

The running-dog motif is self-explanatory. Each corner is shown as it differs from the other corners.

When you have done one sequence of the rotation of the motifs and triangles, it will be easy to get the correct colors for the borders, backgrounds, and centers.

Total number of skeins of 7/2 wool needed: 102

Pile material: 7/2 wool doubled

Heading: 12/9 fishnet twine loose

Warp: 12/9 fishnet twine, eight pairs per horizontal inch (431 pairs, including 4 for selvage)

Weft: 30/9 fishnet twine loose and 30/9 under tension

Selvage: 7/2 wool doubled

Height of pile: 1/4 inch

Overall size: 54 x 47 inches

Type of knots: Ghiordes, 12.5 per vertical inch (591 rows of vertical knots)

Colors (listed in order of predominant use, background may be maroon or dark brown):

☐ 7/2 maroon #3027 or 7/2 dark brown #3018
☒ 7/2 red # 3024
◎ 7/2 dark blue #3013
▽ 7/2 dark green #3030
▣ 7/2 gold #3036
⦿ 7/2 black #3099
△ 7/2 honey beige #3303

Table 3

Motif	Outline	Background	Cross in Center	Center of Cross
1	Dark green	Red	Dark green	Maroon
2	Red	Dark blue	Red	Beige
3	Dark blue	Maroon	Dark blue	Maroon
4	Red	Dark green	Maroon	Beige

Design 8. *Talish rug* (plate H)

Several adaptations can be made with this lovely rug. It has the bright colors of most Caucasian rugs. The diagonal rows of stars in the center are particularly appealing. An equally beautiful Talish rug can be made with a solid navy blue center with no designs in it. Instead of spending the 800 hours that it took me to make this rug, you can make a rug a little shorter just by picking a point past the major design and ending the rug there. Anything from a square mat to a rug approximately 6½ feet long can be made from this design. It is possible to make four or five rugs varying the colors or the length of the design as shown here. From the color plate you can see the color sequence in the rows of stars.

Total number of skeins of 7/2 wool needed: 113½

Pile material: 7/2 wool doubled

Heading: 12/6 fishnet twine, loose

Warp: 12/6 fishnet twine, ten pairs per horizontal inch (405 pairs, including 4 for selvage)

Weft: 12/6 fishnet twine loose and 12/6 under tension

Selvage: 7/2 wool doubled, red color

Height of pile: ⅜ inch

Overall size: 40 x 78 inches

Type of knots: Ghiordes, nine to ten per vertical inch (701 vertical rows of knots)

The instructions above apply if you have made a 58-inch loom as suggested in Chapter 1. You can make this Talish rug on your smaller loom, but you will need to follow the same warp and weft relationships as described under the Kashan rug. You will end up with fourteen knots per horizontal inch and thirteen knots per vertical inch.

Colors (listed in order of predominant use):

- ⊠ 7/2 red #3024
- ☑ 7/2 medium blue #3022
- ◎ 7/2 natural beige #3001
- ⊞ 7/2 yellow #3003
- ⊡ 7/2 dark brown #3018
- ⫼ 7/2 dark blue #3013
- △ 7/2 light green #3008
- ⊡ 7/2 tan #3302
- ⫽ 7/2 gold #3036
- ⟍ 7/2 silver beige #3304

The outlining colors, colors of the motifs, and interior design colors are clearly visible in the color plate:

1. Refer to the corner designs for details of the border guard. In the first minor border, each corner is different.

2. The second minor border from the outside contains the figures that look like small British flags. There are sixteen such figures on the red background, which is 355 knots wide. Allow two red knots on the outside of the first and last figures. That leaves nine spaces of seven knots each and six spaces of eight knots each between the figures.

Lengthwise there are thirty-four "British flags" in the second minor border, with two red knots at the upper and lower ends of the series of figures. That leaves twenty-two spaces of six red knots and eleven spaces of seven red knots between the thirty-four figures. Make notations of how many of each spacing you are using, and the figures will come out right at the end.

3. In the major border with beige background see the design on the graph for spacing across the ends of the rug. Vertically the spacing is the same except that every third spacing is six beige knots instead of five.

4. The inner border with the "British flags" is the same as the outer border of the same design except for spacing. Going across the rug there are six spaces of eight knots and two spaces of seven knots between the nine figures. Lengthwise there are twenty-four spaces of six knots and two spaces of five knots between the twenty-seven figures.

5. The spacing between the stars in the center can be obtained from the design. The colors of the diagonal rows of stars and other minor borders are likewise to be obtained by referring to the color plate.

6. In the yellow minor border the spacing of the diamond shaped figures is as indicated on the graph. Some minor adjustments will be needed toward the end of the rug to make the figure come out right.

Design 9. *Kashan rug* (plate I)

The Kashan design is a very lovely vase of flowers on a dark blue background. The braided pink, red, and dark green design in the major border is, I think, rather unusual. This rug is one of the first ones I made with deeply depressed warp threads. If one had the time and patience to make a pair of these, they would be a beautiful addition to any home. You will need a Turkish or Persian daftoon to make this rug. The thin weft must be held at a 45-degree angle as it is inserted in small bubbles with a crochet hook. If this is not done, the rows of knots will be held apart by the weft and the sides of the rug will pull in.

Total number of skeins of 7/2 wool needed: 24

Pile material: 7/2 wool single strand

Heading: 12/6 fishnet twine loose

Warp: 12/6 fishnet twine, fourteen pairs per horizontal inch (324 pairs, including 4 for selvage)

Weft: 16/2 cotton doubled inserted loosely and 1.5 mm Haitian cotton under tension (any soft, loosely spun cotton twine about 1.5 mm in diameter may be used)

Selvage: 7/2 wool doubled, same color as border

Height of pile: ¼ inch

Overall size: 23 x 28 inches

Type of knots: Senna, thirteen per vertical inch (365 vertical rows of knots)

The Kashan pattern is in three panels: The first panel is the lower one-third of the rug, the second the middle one-third, and the third the upper one-third. Please note that the corner design is different in the upper and lower corners on the right side of the rug. Also, one part of the chain across the upper and lower border is different from the rest of the chain (near midportion).

Colors (listed in order of predominant use):

☐ 7/2 dark blue #3013
☒ 7/2 red #3024
⊡ 7/2 pink #3017
⊞ 7/2 gold #3036
⊽ 7/2 dark green #3030
△ 7/2 honey beige #3303
⊡ 7/2 natural beige #3001
⫿⫿ 7/2 medium green #3010
⫿ 7/2 medium blue #3022
▢ 7/2 dark brown #3018

When tying the heddles, be sure that the first back warp is pulled forward to the left of the first left front warp. This ensures that the last warp on the right side of the rug will be a front one. Thus the encircled warp will be a front warp and will lie on the surface of the rug.

A. *Shiraz mat (Design 1)*

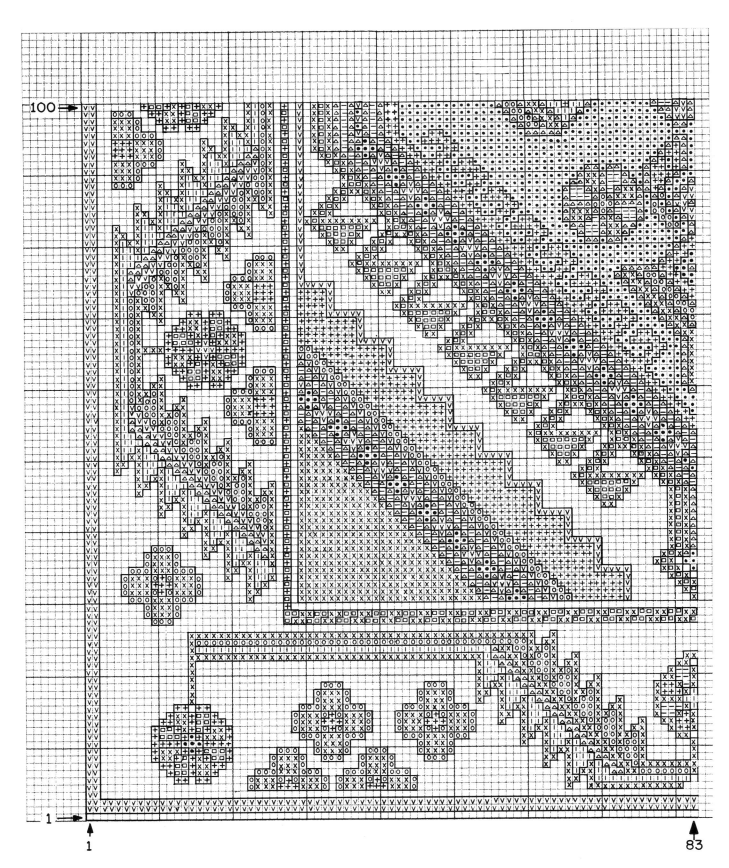

1A. Shiraz mat (bottom)

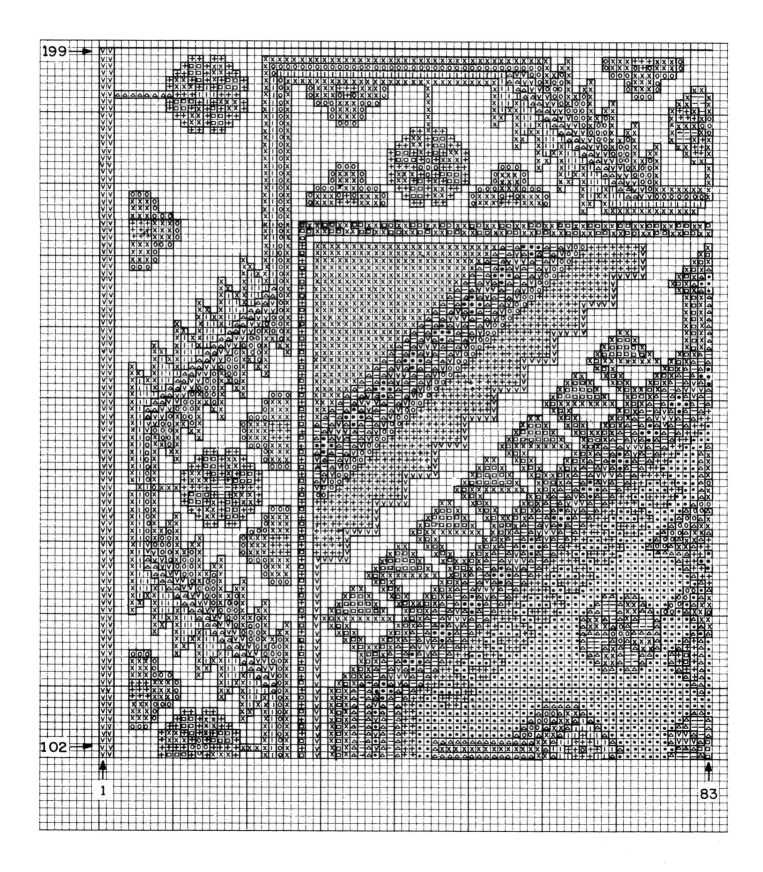

1B. Shiraz mat (top)

B. *Gendje mat (Design 2)*

1

2. Gendje mat

c. Albuturkey rug (Design 3)

3A. Albuturkey rug

3B. Albuturkey rug (right border and corner)

D. *Shiraz mat (Design 4)*

1

1

4A. Shiraz mat (left side)

4B. Shiraz mat (right side)

E. *Chinese rug (Design 5)*

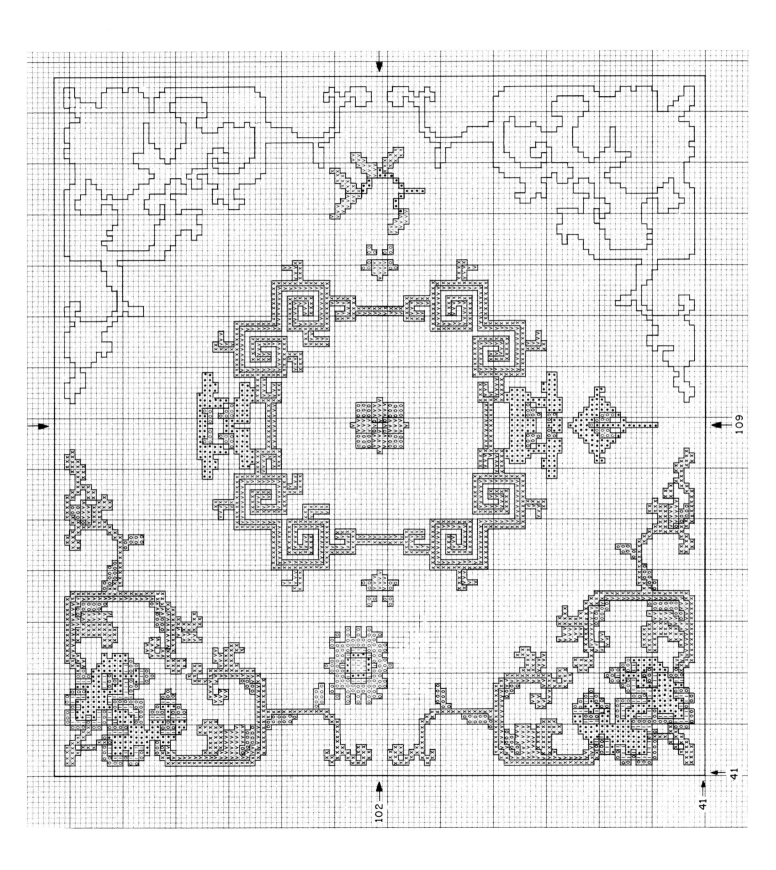

5A. Chinese rug (center)

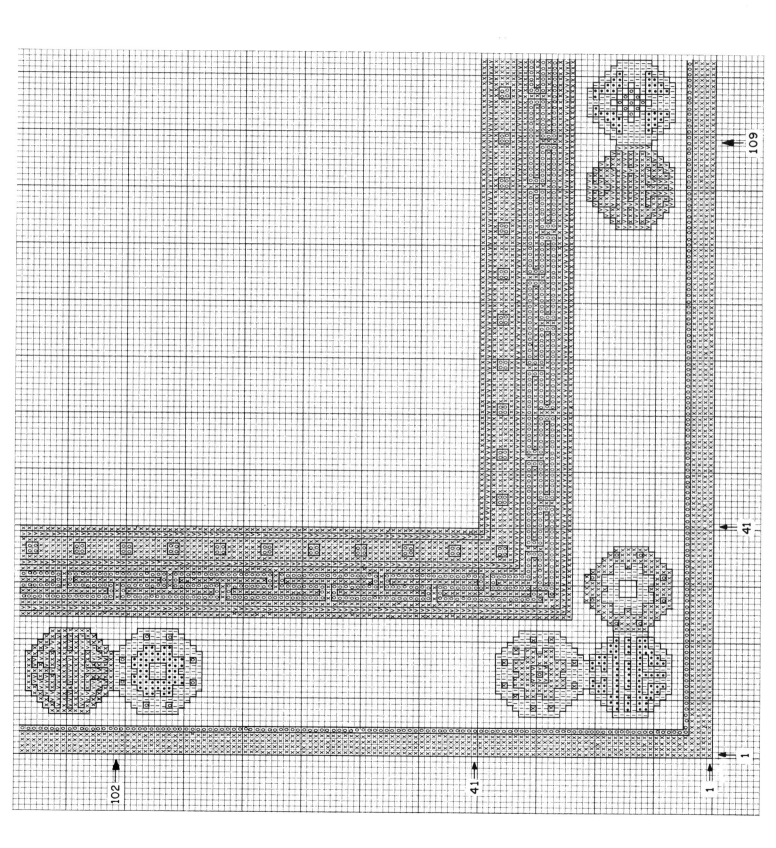

5B. Chinese rug (left border)

F. *Qashgai duck rug (Design 6)*

211 →

91 →

42

82

6A. Qashgai duck rug (center)

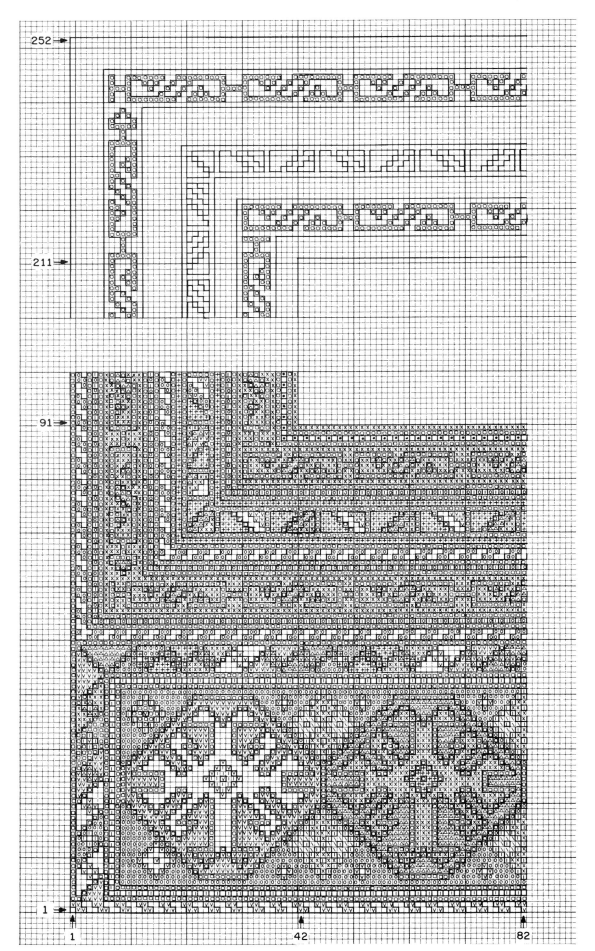

6B. Qashgai duck rug (left side, bottom)

6C. Qashgai duck rug (right side, bottom)

G. *Yomud Turkoman bag face (Design 7)*

7A. Yomud Turkoman bag face (center)

348 →

185 →

60   112   163

7B. Yomud Turkoman bag face (bottom)

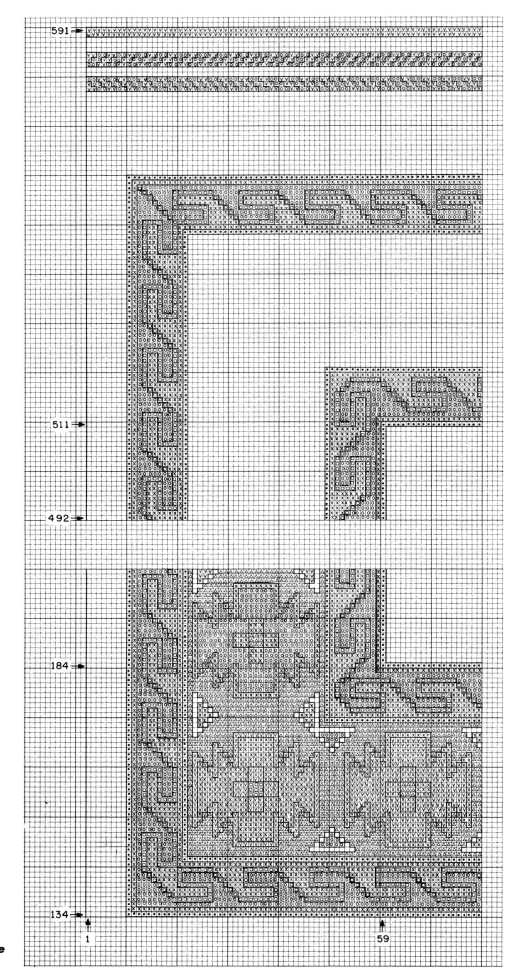

**7C. Yomud Turkoman bag face
(upper and lower left border)**

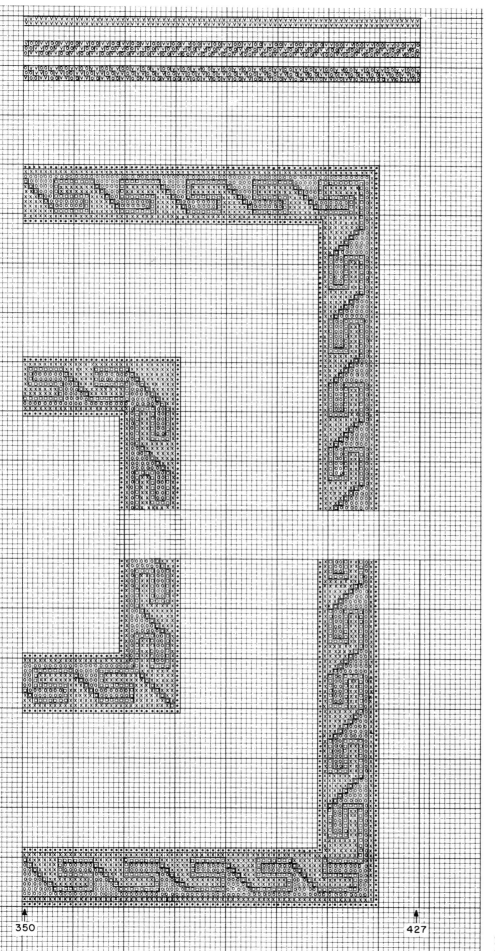

350

427

**7D. Yomud Turkoman bag face
(upper and lower right border)**

H. *Talish rug (Design 8)*

127 →

1 →

1

8A. Talish rug (lower left border)

100

8B. Talish rug (center)

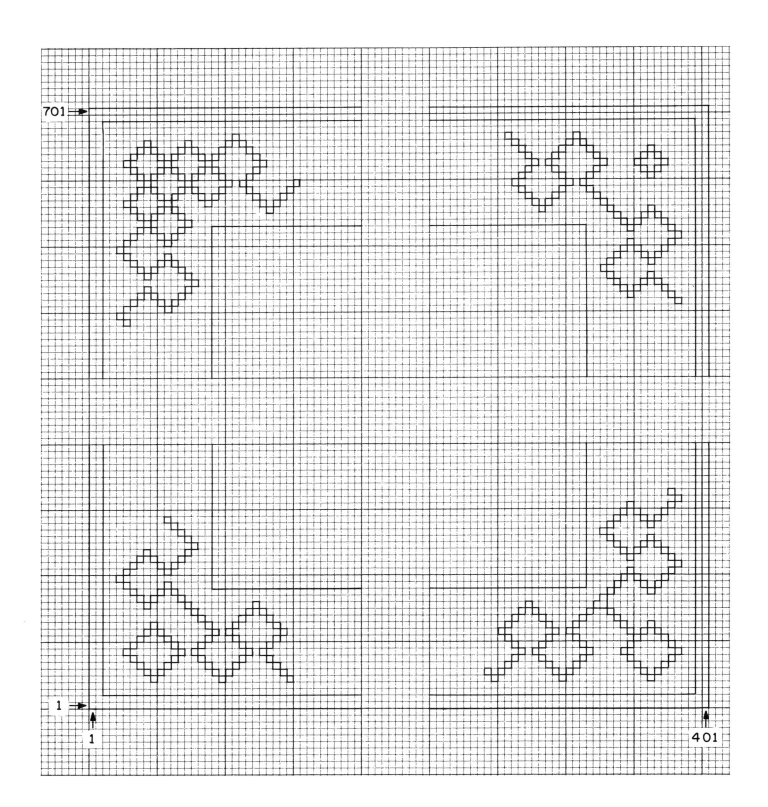

701

1

1

1

401

8C. Talish rug (corners of outer border)

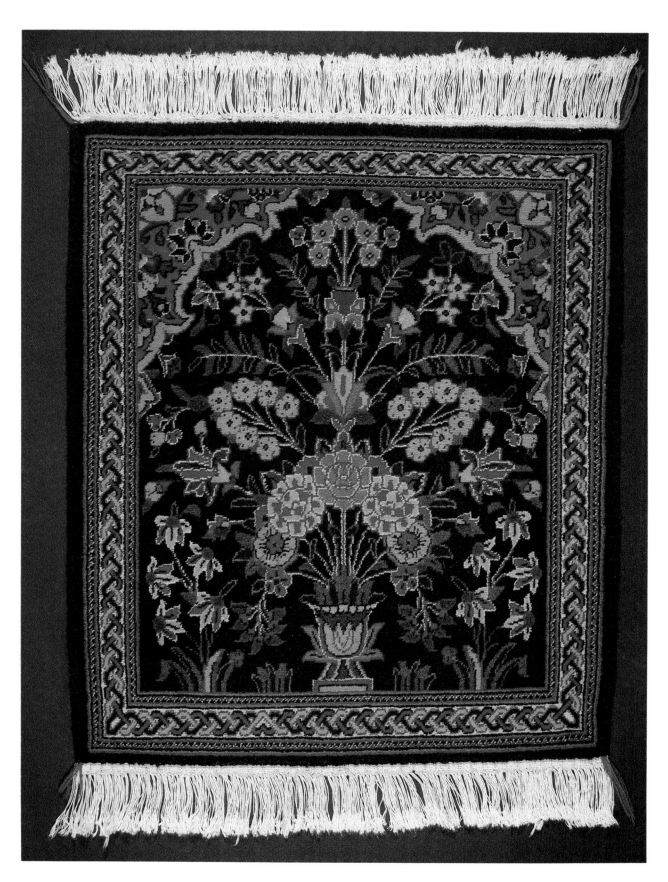

I. *Kashan rug (Design 9)*

A

9A. Kashan rug (lower panel, left)

1

80

A

9B. Kashan rug (lower panel, center)

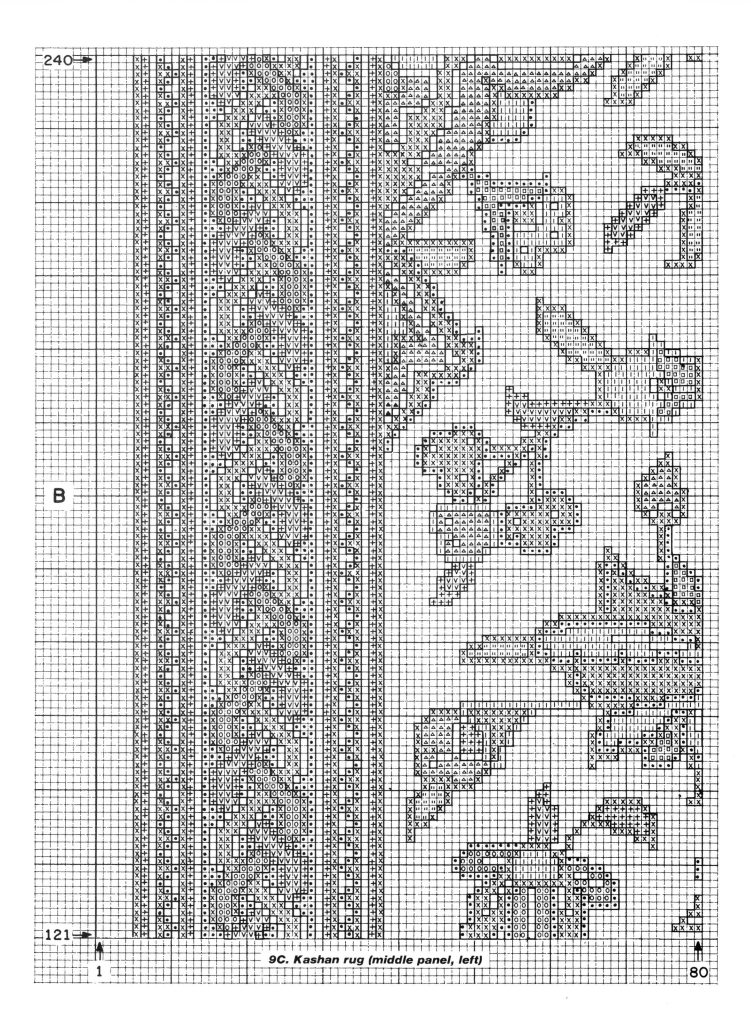

B

1

9C. Kashan rug (middle panel, left)

80

B

9D. Kashan rug (middle panel, center)

160

121

C

9E. Kashan rug (upper panel, left)

1

80

C

241

9F. Kashan rug (upper panel, center)

81

160

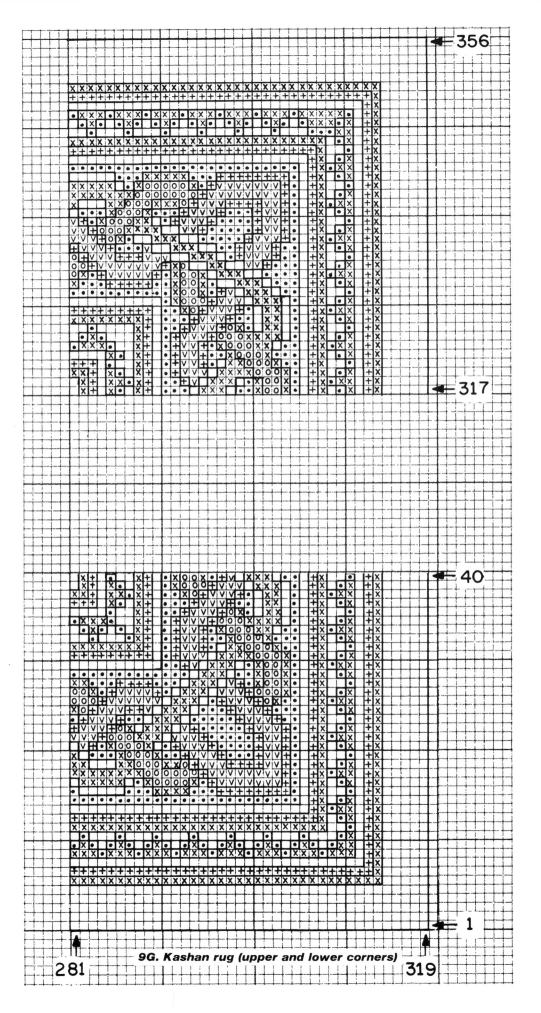

9G. Kashan rug (upper and lower corners)

Sources

Because the Scandinavian yarns referred to in this book are infrequently used by American weavers, most wool stores will not have them in stock. School Products, Inc. acts as a principal importer for these weaving supplies; they also stock other essential tools and supplies you will need. You may order the wool directly from them or through your local wool or craft shop.

Village Wools has agreed to stock a modest inventory of these supplies because of the special interest in knotted pile weaving in New Mexico, the author's home state.

For finer rugs, such as the one shown in plate I, you will need a metal daftoon from the Middle East. If you have a Turkish friend, he could probably get one for you from Turkey. Just show him the photograph in this book (fig. 17). Also ask him to get you some angled rug scissors (fig. 22).

School Products, Inc., 1201 Broadway, New York, New York 10001
Klippans tuna garn 7/2
Klippans blue cotton 16/2
Fishnet twine
Navajo warp
LeClerc umbrella swift
LeClerc weighted rug comb
WASA carpet scissors

Village Wools, 3801 C. San Mateo, N.E., Albuquerque, New Mexico 87110
Klippans tuna garn 7/2
Klippans blue cotton 16/2
Harrisville 2-ply wool
Fishnet twine
Navajo warp
Haitian cotton
LeClerc umbrella swift
LeClerc weighted rug comb
WASA carpet scissors

LeClerc Corporation, P.O. Box 491, Plattsburgh, New York 12901
Weighted rug comb
Umbrella swift

Waldmin and Saam (WASA), 565 Solingen-Weyer, Gottlieb-Heinrich-Strasse 1, Germany
5½-inch carpet scissors

Knadjian's Rugs and Carpets, 1418 Central Avenue, S.E., Albuquerque, New Mexico 87106
Persian metal rug comb (daftoon)

Davidson's Old Mill, Eaton Rapids, Michigan 48827
Navajo warp

John Snyder, 12509 Towner, N.E., Albuquerque, New Mexico 87104
Will build looms for weavers in the Albuquerque, New Mexico area.

The Quilt Works, 11117 Menaul, N.E., Albuquerque, New Mexico 87112
Leather thimbles

The Nifty Needle, 7122 Menaul, N.E., Albuquerque, New Mexico 87110
Paterna 3-ply wool

World of Knives:
1050 Coronado Shopping Center, N.E., Albuquerque, New Mexico 87110
Preston Wood Town Center, 5301 Beltline, Space 2104, Dallas, Texas 75240
2201 Kalahaua Avenue, Honolulu, Hawaii 96815
4471 Mall of Memphis, Suite 2, Memphis, Tennessee 38118
Town and Country Shopping Center, 800 Westbelt, Suite J-189, Houston, Texas 77024
WASA carpet scissors
Wiss carpet scissors

Weaving Works, 5049 Brooklyn N.E., Seattle,
Washington 98008
CUM 7/2
Marks tuna garn
Berga filtgarn
Harrisville yarns
Navajo warp
LeClerc beater
LeClerc shuttle
Fishnet twine
Swifts
Persian needlepoint yarns
Carpet scissors

Further Reading

Bamborough, Philip. *Antique Oriental Rugs and Carpets*.
    Poole, Dorset, England: Blandford Press, 1979.
Bennett, Ian. *Rugs and Carpets of the World*. New York:
    A and W Publishers, 1977.
Eiland, Murray L. *Chinese and Exotic Rugs*. Boston: New
    York Graphic Society, 1979.
_____. *Oriental Rugs: A Comprehensive Guide*. Revised
    edition. Boston: New York Graphic Society, 1976.
Formenton, Fabio. *Oriental Rugs and Carpets*. New York:
    McGraw-Hill, 1972.
Gregorian, Arthur T. *Oriental Rugs and the Stories They
    Tell*. New York: Charles Scribner's Sons, 1967.
Herbert, Janice Summers. *Affordable Oriental Rugs*. New
    York: Macmillan, 1980.
Jacobsen, Charles W. *Oriental Rugs: A Complete Guide*.
    Rutland, Vermont: Charles E. Tuttle Company, 1972.
Kendrick, A. F., and Tattersall, C. E. C. *Hand-Woven
    Carpets, Oriental and European*. New York: Dover,
    1973.
Kline, Linda. *Beginner's Guide to Oriental Rugs*. Berkeley,
    California: Ross Books, 1980.
Lane, Maggie. *Needlepoint by Design*. New York: Charles
    Scribner's Sons, 1970.
_____. *More Needlepoint by Design*. New York: Charles
    Scribner's Sons, 1972.
_____. *Rugs and Wall Hangings*. New York: Charles
    Scribner's Sons, 1976.
Milhofer, Stefan A. *The Color Treasury of Oriental Rugs*.
    New York: Thomas Y. Crowell Company, 1976.
Schürmann, Ulrich. *Oriental Carpets*. London: Octopus
    Books Limited, 1979.
Tattersall, C. E. C. *Notes on Proper Knotting and Weaving*.
    Monograph available through the Textile Museum,
    2320 South Washington Street, N.W., Washington,
    D.C. 20008.

Index

Selected Books from Pacific Search Press